Appalachian Trail Guide to New York–New Jersey

Appalachian Trail Guide to
New York–New Jersey

New York–New Jersey Trail Conference

Daniel D. Chazin
Field Editor

FIFTEENTH EDITION

Appalachian Trail Conference
HARPERS FERRY

Guidebook Contributors

Daniel D. Chazin, Editor

Jill Arbuckle

Mike Arthur

Bob Boyle

Walt Daniels

Ronald J. Dupont, Jr.

Jane Geisler

Gordon Greacen

Jim Haggett

Karen Lutz

Gail Neffinger

Michael Rea

Ron Rosen

Robert Sickley III

Glenn Scherer

Larry Wheelock

Cover photo, © C.W. Banfield
© 2002, New York–New Jersey Trail Conference, Mahwah, New Jersey
Published by The Appalachian Trail Conference, Harpers Ferry, West Virginia

Please see page 273 for photography credits.

ISBN 1-889386-32-4

Fifteenth Edition
Printed in the United States of America on recycled paper.

The diamond Trail marker on the previous page is a registered servicemark of the Appalachian Trail Conference. All rights reserved.

Contents

About the Appalachian Trail

Welcome to the America's best-known long-distance footpath, the Appalachian Trail. If you've never visited it before, you're in for a memorable time, and we hope this official guidebook will help you make the most of it. If you know the Trail, but not this part of it, we hope this book will help you discover new aspects of an experience that changes from state to state, mile to mile, and season to season.

Not long after the end of World War I, a Massachusetts forester and dreamer named Benton MacKaye envisioned a footpath running along the crests of the eastern mountains, from New England to the southern Appalachians. The work of thousands of volunteers helped that dream become the Appalachian Trail, which, as of 2002, extended 2,169 miles between Katahdin, in central Maine, and Springer Mountain, in northern Georgia. Its terrain ranges from swampland bog bridges to near-vertical rock scrambles that challenge the fittest wilderness trekker; its white "blazes" lead from busy small-town streets to remote mountain ridges, days from the nearest road crossing.

The "A.T.," as it's called by hikers, is a linear trail that can be enjoyed in small pieces or large chunks. Hikers follow its blazes on round-trip day-hikes, on loop-hikes (where side-trails connect with it and form a loop), on one-way "section-hikes" or overnight backpacking trips that cover short or long segments, or on end-to-end "thru-hikes" that cover the entire Trail. It is continuously marked, using a standard system of paint blazes and signs, and is cleared of undergrowth and maintained to permit single-file hiking. (Bicycles, horses, and motorized vehicles are not permitted along most of the route.) Many campsites and more than 250 primitive woodland shelters are located along the Trail, typically about a day's hike apart. The path itself is usually dirt, or rock, or grass, and only very short segments are paved or wheelchair-accessible.

Maine

Vt.

N.H.

New York

Mass.

R

Conn.

Mich.

N.J.

Pennsylvania

Ohio

Md.

D e l.

W. Va.

Kentucky

Virginia

Atlantic
Ocean

Tenn.

North
Carolina

South
Carolina

Georgia

100   N   100 Miles
0

This remarkable footpath is much more than just a walk through the woods. When it was first begun in the 1920s and completed in the 1930s, it was little-known and rarely traveled. Large parts of it were on private property. Since 1968, it has been a part of the same national park system that includes Yellowstone, Yosemite, and the Great Smoky Mountains. Its official name today is the Appalachian National Scenic Trail, and 99 percent of it runs over public lands. Hundreds of roads cross it, and hundreds of side trails intersect with it. In some parts, the Trail "corridor" is only a few hundred feet wide; in other parts, entire mountains are protected by it.

Unlike other well-known national parks, there's no "main entrance" to the A.T., with a gate and a ranger collecting tickets. You can begin or end your hike at hundreds of places between its northern and southern ends. As the longest, skinniest part of America's national park system, the A.T. stretches across fourteen different states and passes through more than sixty federal, state, and local parks and forests. Maybe the most important difference between the A.T. and other national-park units, though, is that it was built by volunteers, and volunteers still are responsible for keeping it up.

Appalachian Trail Conference headquarters

The A.T. relies on a system known as "cooperative management" rather than on a large, paid federal staff. Yes, there are a handful of National Park Service staff members and a ranger assigned to the Appalachian Trail Park Office in Harpers Ferry, West Virginia, but thousands of the people who maintain, patrol, and monitor the footpath and its surrounding lands are outdoor lovers like you. Each year, as members of thirty-one "maintaining clubs" up and down the Appalachians, they volunteer hundreds of thousands of hours of their time looking after this public treasure. They would welcome your help.

About the Appalachian Trail Conference—We are the volunteer-based organization that teaches people about the Trail, coordinates the work of the maintaining clubs, and works with the government agencies, individuals, and companies that own the land that the Trail passes over. The membership of the Appalachian Trail Conference (ATC) includes more than 33,000 hikers and Trail enthusiasts, who elect a volunteer Board of Managers every two years. Members' dues and contributions help support a paid staff of about forty people at the ATC headquarters in Harpers Ferry and at field offices in New Hampshire, Pennsylvania, Virginia, and North Carolina. Our World Wide Web site, <www.appalachiantrail.org>, is a good source of information about the Trail. Information about contacting the Conference is on page 274 in the back of this book.

Tips for enjoying
the Appalachian Trail

Follow the blazes—The Appalachian Trail is marked for daylight travel in both directions, using a system of paint "blazes" on trees, posts, and rocks. There are some local variations, but most hikers grasp the system quickly. Above treeline, and where snow or fog may obscure paint marks, posts and rock piles called "cairns" are used to identify the route.

A blaze is a rectangle of paint in a prominent place along a trail. White-paint blazes two inches wide and six inches high mark the A.T. itself. Side trails and shelter trails use blue blazes; blazes of other colors and shapes mark intersecting trails. Two white blazes, one above the other, signal an obscure turn, route change, incoming side trail, or other situation that requires you to be especially alert to changes in direction. In some states, one of the two blazes will be offset in the direction of the turn.

If you have gone a quarter-mile without seeing a blaze, stop. Retrace your steps until you locate a blaze. Then, check to ensure that you haven't missed a turn. Often a glance backward will reveal blazes meant for hikers traveling in the opposite direction.

White blaze

Double blaze

Volunteer Trail maintainers regularly relocate small sections of the path around hazards, undesirable features, or off private property. When your map or guidebook indicates one route, and the blazes show another, follow the blazes.

Leave No Trace—As more and more people use the Trail and other backcountry areas, it becomes more important to learn to enjoy wild places without ruining them. The best way to do this is to understand and practice the principles of Leave No Trace, a seven-point ethic for enjoying the backcountry that applies to everything from a picnic outing to a long-distance expedition. Leave No Trace is also a nonprofit organization dedicated to teaching the principles of low-impact use. For more information, contact Leave No Trace at <www.lnt.org>, or call (800) 332-4100.

The seven principles of the Leave No Trace ethic are:

1. *Plan ahead and prepare.* Evaluate the risks associated with your outing, identify campsites and destinations in advance, use maps and guides, and be ready for bad weather. When people don't plan ahead, they're more likely to damage the backcountry.

2. *Travel and camp on durable surfaces.* Stay on trails and don't bushwhack short-cuts across switchbacks or other bends in the

Post

Cairn

path. Keep off fragile trailside areas, such as bogs or alpine zones. Camp in designated spots, such as shelters and existing campsites, so that unspoiled areas aren't trampled and denuded.

3. *Dispose of waste properly.* Bury or pack out excrement, including pet droppings. Pack out all trash and food waste, including that left behind by others. Don't bury trash or food, and don't try to burn packaging materials in campfires.

4. *Leave what you find.* Don't take flowers or other sensitive natural resources. Don't disturb artifacts such as native American arrowheads or the stone walls and cellar holes of historical woodland homesteads.

5. *Minimize campfire impacts.* Campfires are enjoyable, but they also create the worst visual and ecological impact of any backcountry camping practice. If possible, cook on a backpacking stove instead of a fire. Where fires are permitted, build them only in established fire rings, and don't add rocks to an existing ring. Keep fires small. Burn only dead and downed wood that can be broken by hand—leave axes and saws at home. Never leave your campfire unattended, and drown it when you leave.

6. *Respect wildlife.* Don't feed or disturb wildlife. Store food properly to avoid attracting bears, varmints, and rodents. If you bring a pet, keep it leashed.

7. *Be considerate of other visitors.* Limit overnight groups to ten or fewer, twenty-five on day trips. Minimize noise and intrusive behavior. Share shelters and other facilities. Be considerate of Trail neighbors.

A few cautions—The A.T. is a scenic trail through the forests of the Appalachian Mountains. It is full of natural splendors and is fun to hike, and parts of it run near roads and across fairly level ground. But, most of the Trail is very steep and runs deep in the woods, along the crests of rocky mountain ridges, miles from the nearest houses or paved roads. It will test your physical conditioning and skills. Plan your hike, and prepare sensibly.

Before you set out to hike the Trail, take a few minutes to review the information in this guidebook. It is as current as possible, but conditions and footpath locations sometimes change in between guidebook editions. On the Trail, please pay close attention to—and follow—the blazes and any directional signs that mark the route, even if the book describes a different route.

Although we have included some basic tips for preparing for an A.T. hike in the back of this guidebook (see page 220), this is not a "how-to" guide to backpacking. Many good books of that sort are available in your local bookstore and library. If you've never hiked before, we recommend that you take the time to read one or two and to research equipment, camping techniques, and trip planning. If your only hiking and camping experience is in local parks and forests, be aware that hiking and camping in the mountains can be extremely strenuous and disorienting and has its own particular challenges. You will sometimes encounter wildlife and will have to make do with primitive (or nonexistent) sanitary facilities. Remember that water in the backcountry, even at water sources mentioned in this guidebook, needs to be treated for microorganisms before you drink it.

Responsibility for safety—Finally, know that you are responsible for your own safety, for the safety of those with you, and for making sure that your food and water are safe for consumption. Hiking the A.T. is no more dangerous than many other popular outdoor activities, but, although the Trail is part of the national park system, it is not the proverbial "walk in the park." The Appalachian Trail Conference and its member maintaining clubs cannot ensure the safety of any hiker on the Trail; as a hiker, you assume the risk for any accident, illness, or injury that might occur there.

How to use this book

We suggest that you use this book in conjunction with the waterproof trail maps that were sold with it. Certain maps can be purchased separately from the guidebook, but not for all sections of the Trail. Information about services available in towns near the Trail is updated annually in the *Appalachian Trail Thru-Hikers' Companion*. Mileage and shelter information for the entire Trail are updated annually in the *Appalachian Trail Data Book*.

Although the Trail is usually well marked, and experienced hikers may be able to follow it without either guidebook or map, using the book and the maps will not only help you keep from getting lost or disoriented, but will also help you get more out of your hike.

Before you start your hike:

- *Decide where you want to go and which Trail features you hope to see.* Use the book to help you plan your trip. The chapter on "Suggested Day Trips" (page 216 below) lists a number of popular day-hikes and short trips that have proven popular with hikers along this part of the Trail. The introductions to each section give more detail, summarizing scenic and cultural highlights along the route that you may wish to visit.

- *Calculate mileage for linear or loop hikes.* Each chapter lists mileage between landmarks on the route, along with details to help you follow the path. Use the mileage and descriptions to determine how far you must hike, how long it will take you, and where you can camp if you're taking an overnight or long-distance hike.

- *Find the Trail.* Use the road maps included in the guidebook to locate parking areas near the A.T. and the "Trailheads" or "road crossings" where the footpath crosses the highway. In some cases, the guidebook includes directions to nearby towns and commercial areas where you can find food, supplies, and lodging.

After you begin hiking:

- *Identify landmarks.* Deduce where you are along the Trail by comparing the descriptions in the guidebook and the features on the waterproof maps to the landscape you're hiking through. Much of the time, the Trail's blazes will lead you through seemingly featureless woodlands, where the only thing you can see in most directions is trees, but periodically you will be able to check your progress at viewpoints, meadows, mountain tops, stream crossings, road crossings, and Trailside structures.

- *Learn about the route.* Native Americans, colonial-era settlers, Civil War soldiers, nineteenth-century farmers, pioneering railroaders, and early industrial entrepreneurs explored these hills long before the A.T. was built. Although much of what they left behind has long since been overgrown and abandoned, your guidebook will point out old settlements and forest roads and put the landscape in its historical context. It will touch on the geology, natural history, and modern-day ecosystems of the eastern mountains.

- *Find campsites and side trails.* The guidebook includes directions to other trails, as well as creeks, mountain springs, and established tenting and shelter sites.

Areas covered

Each of the eleven official Appalachian Trail guidebooks describes several hundred miles of the Trail. In some cases, that includes a single state, such as Maine or Pennsylvania. In other cases, the guidebook may include several states, such as the one covering northern Virginia, West Virginia, and Maryland. Because so much of the Trail is in Virginia (more than 500 miles of it), a hiker needs to use four different guidebooks to cover that entire state.

The eleven guidebooks are:

Maine
New Hampshire–Vermont
Massachusetts–Connecticut
New York–New Jersey
Pennsylvania
Maryland and Northern Virginia
Shenandoah National Park
Central Virginia
Southwest Virginia
Tennessee–North Carolina
North Carolina–Georgia

How the guidebook is divided

Rather than trying to keep track of several hundred miles of the Trail from beginning to end, the Trail's maintainers break it down into smaller "sections." Each section typically covers the area between important road crossings or natural features and can vary from three to thirty miles in length. A typical section is from five to fifteen miles long. This guidebook is organized according to those sections, beginning with the northernmost in the coverage area and ending with the southernmost. Each section makes up a chapter. A summary of distances for the entire guidebook appears at the end of the book.

How sections are organized

Brief description of section—Each section begins with a brief description of the route. The description mentions highlights and prominent features and gives a sense of what it's like to hike the section as a whole.

Section map and profile—The map shows how to find the Trail from your car (it is not a detailed map and should not be relied on for navigating the Trail) and includes notable roads along with a rough depiction of the Trail route, showing shelter locations. A schematic profile of the high and low points in the section gives you an idea of how much climbing or descending is ahead.

Shelters and campsites—Each chapter also includes an overview of shelters and campsites for the section, including the distances between shelters and information about water supplies. Along some parts of the Trail, particularly north of the Mason-Dixon Line, the designated sites are the only areas in which camping is permitted. In other parts of the Trail, even where "dispersed camping" is allowed, we recommend that hikers "Leave No Trace" (see page 7) and reduce their impact on the Trail's resources by using established campsites. If camping is restricted in a section, it will be noted here.

Trail description—Trail descriptions appear on the right-hand pages of each chapter. Although the description reads from north to south, it is organized for both northbound and southbound hikers. North-bound hikers should start at the end of the chapter and read up, using the mileages in the right-hand column. Southbound hikers should read down, using the mileages in the left-hand column. The descrip-

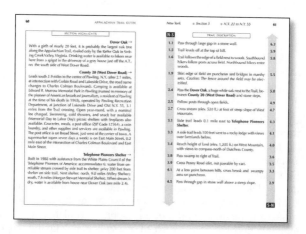

tion includes obvious landmarks you will pass, though it may not include all stream crossings, summits, or side-trails. Where the Trail route becomes confusing, the guide will provide both north- and southbound directions from the landmark. When a feature appears in **bold** type, it means that you should see the section highlights for more detail.

Section highlights—On the left-hand pages of each chapter, you will find cultural, historical, natural, and practical information about the **bold** items in the Trail description. That includes detailed information about Trailheads, shelters, and campsites, along with notes on the historical and cultural resources of the route, notes on landforms and natural history, and descriptions of sidetrails.

End of section—The northern and southern ends of each section are noted in **bold** in the Trail description and detailed in the section highlights at the beginning and ending of each chapter of the book, respectively. The information includes brief directions about how to find the Trailhead from the highway, information about where to park, if parking is available, distances to nearby towns and facilities, and notes on the services available near the Trail, such as grocery stores and restaurants.

Guidebook conventions

North or "compass-north"?—For the sake of convenience, the directions *north, south, east* and *west* in the guide refer to the general north–south orientation of the Trail, rather than the true north or magnetic north of maps and charts. In other words, when a hiker is northbound on the Trail, whatever is to his left will be referred to as "west" and whatever is to the right will be "east." For southbounders, the opposite is true.

Although this is instinctively the way A.T. hikers orient themselves, it can be slightly confusing for the first-time A.T. hiker, since the Trail does not always follow an actual north–south orientation. For example, you might be "northbound" along the Trail (headed toward Maine), but, because of a sharp turn or a switchback up the side of a mountain, your compass will tell you you're actually pointed south for a while. Nevertheless, in this guide, a trail or road intersecting on the left side of the A.T. for the northbound hiker will always be referred to as "intersecting on the west side of the A.T.," even where the compass says otherwise.

When the compass direction of an object is important, as when directing attention to a certain feature seen from a viewpoint, the guidebook will refer to "compass-north," "compass-west," and so forth.

Undocumented features—The separate waterproof hiking maps meant to accompany this guide generally reflect all the landmarks discussed here. Because the maps are extremely detailed, some features that appear on them, such as streams and old woods roads, may not be mentioned in the guidebook if they are not important landmarks. Other side trails that the hiker encounters may not be mentioned or mapped at all; in general, this is because the unmarked trails lead onto private property, and Trail managers wish to discourage their use.

The Appalachian Trail
in New York and New Jersey

The New York–New Jersey Trail Conference—The A.T. between the Connecticut border and the Delaware River is maintained by members of the New York–New Jersey Trail Conference (NY–NJ TC), a nonprofit volunteer organization. Founders of the NY–NJ TC constructed the first section of the A.T. when, in 1923, they opened a section in Harriman and Bear Mountain state parks in New York. Today, through a network of eighty-five hiking and environmental organizations and about ten thousand individual members, volunteers continue to maintain the A.T. in New York and New Jersey, as well as other trails.

The NY–NJ TC was formed in 1920 when local hiking clubs gathered to plan a system of marked trails to make Harriman and Bear Mountain state parks more accessible to the public. During the 1930s, more trails were built, and a system of trail maintenance was developed, giving each hiking club a share of the responsibility. Today, this network covers 1,300 miles of marked trails from the Catskills and Taconics south to the Delaware Water Gap.

In addition to maintaining the A.T. in New York and New Jersey and managing federal Trail lands there, the NY–NJ TC has been responsible for relocating the Trail away from roads and unprotected private lands and onto protected woodlands. Of the more than 160 miles of the Trail in the two states, virtually all are now part of a protected corridor of land 800 to 1,000 feet wide. The NY–NJ TC, ATC, and state and federal officials have entered into cooperative agreements and adopted local management plans for the Trail that define the obligations and responsibilities of all parties. The relocations in these two states have made the A.T. through New York and New Jersey a hike you won't want to miss.

New York–New Jersey Trail Conference volunteers devote many hours to other issues affecting the trails and promote programs that support the responsible stewardship of natural resources. They also work to reduce litter and eliminate the illegal use of ATVs along hiking trails, and to prevent inappropriate development that would threaten regional hiking trails. For example, together with other environmental groups and public entities, NY–NJ TC worked to preserve the 20,000-acre Sterling Forest in New York and New Jersey, once threatened by large-scale development, and helped establish Sterling Forest State Park.

NY–NJ TC publications include the *New York Walk Book, New Jersey Walk Book, Guide to the Long Path, Harriman Trails: A Guide and History, Scenes and Walks in the Northern Shawangunks, Circuit Hikes in Northern New Jersey, Day Walker, Hiking Long Island,* and maps for Harriman and Bear Mountain state parks, North Jersey Trails, East Hudson Trails, South Taconic Trails, Kittatinny Trails, West Hudson Trails, Hudson Palisades, Shawangunks, and Catskills. The first five of those map sets cover sections of the A.T. The NY–NJ TC also publishes the *Trail Walker,* a bimonthly newspaper for members that includes information on A.T. relocations in the two states. Members also receive a publications discount.

For further information, write or call the New York–New Jersey Trail Conference, 156 Ramapo Valley Road, Mahwah, NJ 07430; (201) 512-9348; fax, (201) 512-9012. Contact it by electronic mail at *<info@nynjtc.org>*, or visit its World Wide Web site on the Internet at *<www. nynjtc.org>*.

Camping on the A.T. in New York and New Jersey

The Appalachian Trail in New York and New Jersey is a surprisingly wild place, considering its proximity to the most densely populated areas in America. Even so, the Trail's popularity and the narrowness of the A.T. corridor in both states mean that camping is permitted only at designated shelter areas and campsites. The only exception is the Delaware Water Gap National Recreation Area (parts of New Jersey Sections Five and Six), where long-distance hikers may find their own campsites along the Trail, provided they choose a site that is at least half a mile from developed access roads or the boundaries of the national recreation area. Such campsites must be no more than 100 feet from the Trail.

Campfires—Open campfires are not permitted anywhere along the Trail in New Jersey. In New York, open campfires are permitted only at fireplaces at designated shelters and campsites. In both states, campers should use portable backpacking stoves for cooking.

Groups—If you're part of an organized overnight group, please carry tents, and do not monopolize shelters, which solo hikers often depend on. Keep the groups small (eight to ten people, including leaders; twenty-five or fewer for day trips), and keep noise to a minimum between 9:00 p.m. and 7:00 a.m. for the sake of those attempting to sleep. Please cooperate, and consider the needs of others.

Shelters—Shelters (sometimes called lean-tos) are generally three-sided, with open fronts, and usually are spaced less than a day's hike apart. They often have clearings around them in which you can pitch a tent. They may be fitted with bunks or have a wooden floor for sleeping. Water, a privy, and a table or benches are usually nearby; some New York shelters also have fireplaces. If a shelter has a register, please sign it.

Shelters are available on a first-come, first-served basis, for overnight stays only, and may be crowded during the summer. Except in the case of bad weather, injury, or emergency, they are not intended for stays longer than one or two nights. Hunters, fishermen, and other nonhikers should not use the shelters as bases of operation.

The chart on page 21 is a north-to-south list of the shelters and campsites along the A.T. sections in this guidebook.

Bears and other campsite raiders—Bears, porcupines, skunks, raccoons, squirrels, and mice are common along the A.T. in New York and New Jersey and sometimes visit shelters and well-established camping areas—usually after dark. If they smell your food, they'll eat it if they can! Mice inhabit most Trail shelters. Bears are a particular problem at campsites along the Kittatinny Ridge of New Jersey, from

National Park Service, Appalachian Trail Park Office: (304) 535-6278.

Appalachian Trail Conference: Mid-Atlantic Regional Office, (717) 258-5771; main office, Harpers Ferry, W.Va., (304) 535-6331.

New York

Dial 911; if 911 is not available, dial the following local numbers:

Dutchess County: Sheriff, (845) 486-3800; Fire, (845) 486-2081; State Police, (845) 677-7300.

Orange County: Sheriff, (845) 469-5911; Fire, (845) 469-4911; State Police, (845) 344-5300.

Putnam County: Sheriff and Fire, (845) 526-3300; State Police, (845) 677-7300.

> **Park Police, Fahnestock-Hudson Highlands State Park,** (845) 889-4796.

> **Park Police, Harriman and Bear Mountain state parks** (845) 786-2781.

New Jersey

Dial 911; if 911 is not available, dial the following local numbers:

Warren County: (908) 835-2000; State Police, (908) 459-5000.

Sussex County: (973) 579-0875; State Police, (973) 383-1515.

Passaic County: (973) 881-7500; State Police, (973) 785-9412.

Vernon Township: (973) 827-6155.

> **Delaware Water Gap National Recreation Area,** (717) 588-2435.

> **High Point State Park,** (973) 875-4800.

> **Wawayanda State Park,** (973) 853-4462.

> **Worthington State Forest,** (908) 841-9575.

> **Stokes State Forest,** (973) 948-3820.

High Point State Park south, and may be encountered elsewhere along the Trail in the two-state region. Several shelters have been provided with bear-proof boxes or cables for storing food safely. Please use them. Never leave trash in bear boxes.

The best defense against bears and other campsite raiders is preparing and storing food properly. Cook and eat your meals away from your tent or shelter, so food odors do not linger. If no bear box or cable is available, hang your food, cookware, toothpaste, personal hygiene items, and even water bottles (if you use beverage mixes in them) in a sturdy bag from a strong tree branch at least ten feet off the ground and well away from your campsite. Make sure the bag does not dangle too close to the trunk of the tree; black bears are crafty climbers and good reachers. Never feed bears or leave food behind for them. That simply increases the risks to you and the hikers who follow behind you.

TRAIL SECTION	MILES NORTH–SOUTH	MILES SOUTH–NORTH	SHELTER OR CAMPSITE
CT 5	0.4	11.2	Mt. Algo Lean-to
CT 5	8.6	3.0	Ten Mile River Campsite
CT 5	8.8	2.8	Ten Mile River Lean-to
NY 2	1.2	159.7	Wiley Shelter
NY 3	10.2	150.7	Telephone Pioneers Shelter
NY 4	17.8	143.1	Morgan Stewart Memorial Shelter
NY 6	26.8	134.1	RPH Shelter
NY 6	28.1	132.8	Shenandoah Tenting Area
NY 6	33.8	127.1	Fahnestock State Park campsites *1.0 mile NE of Trail*
NY 7	37.5	123.4	Dennytown Road *group campsites*
NY 9	49.8	111.1	Hemlock Springs Campsite
NY 10	57.8	103.1	West Mountain Shelter *0.6 mile on side trail*
NY 10	60.9	100.0	William Brien Memorial Shelter
NY 11	66.2	94.7	Fingerboard Shelter
NY 12	80.5	80.4	Wildcat Shelter
NJ 1	92.5	68.4	Wawayanda Shelter
NJ 2	104.3	56.6	Pochuck Mountain Shelter
NJ 3	116.7	44.2	High Point Shelter
NJ 4	121.0	39.9	Rutherford Shelter *0.4 mile on side trail*
NJ 4	123.9	37.0	Mashipacong Shelter
NJ 4	129.7	31.2	Gren Anderson Shelter *0.1 mile on side trail*
NJ 5	136.3	24.6	Brink Road Shelter *0.2 mile on side trail*
NJ 6	156.3	4.6	Backpacker Site (no water)

A walk south along the A.T. through New York and New Jersey

The Appalachian Trail crosses the New York–Connecticut state line three times in the 11.5 miles north of New York's Hoyt Road. That section is described in the *Appalachian Trail Guide to Massachusetts–Connecticut,* as well as in this guidebook.

South of Hoyt Road (New York Sections Two through Nine), the Trail enters the Hudson Highlands, passing through Fahnestock State Park and reaching the Hudson River across from Bear Mountain. After crossing the river, it runs generally compass-west through Harriman State Park (New York Sections Ten and Eleven), using a portion of the original route established in 1923. Then it follows the ridges of Bellvale and Bearfort mountains (New York Sections Twelve and Thirteen) west of Greenwood Lake, where it enters New Jersey.

Following a route on a protected corridor acquired largely by the state of New Jersey (New Jersey Sections One through Three), the A.T. traverses the New Jersey Highlands (passing through Wawayanda State Park) and crosses the Great Valley of the Appalachians (through the Wallkill River National Wildlife Refuge), until it reaches high ground again in High Point State Park. There, the Trail turns southward and follows the Kittatinny Ridge on protected land for more than 40 miles through Stokes State Forest (New Jersey Section Four), the Delaware Water Gap National Recreation Area, and Worthington State Forest (New Jersey Sections Five and Six). It crosses the Delaware River on the I-80 toll bridge at the gap.

South of Delaware Water Gap, the Trail is described in the *Appalachian Trail Guide to Pennsylvania.*

Hudson Highlands—The Highlands of New York and New Jersey lie east of the Great Valley of the Appalachians and extend on both sides of the Hudson River, which cuts through them. They are most often referred to as the Hudson Highlands and as the New Jersey Highlands

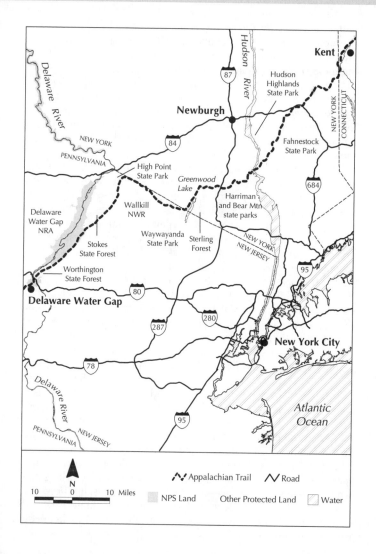

10   N   0   10 Miles   ∿ Appalachian Trail   ∿ Road

NPS Land   Other Protected Land   Water

farther south. It is an area of low mountains and rocky hills that never rise more than 1,500 feet above sea level. Geologically speaking, they are some of the oldest parts of the entire Appalachian Trail. Many of the rocks of the Highlands, and nearby Schaghticoke Mountain in Connecticut, were formed during a mountain-building period that geologists call the Grenville Orogeny, more than one billion years ago. Rock here is typically gneiss, a granite-like "metamorphic" rock formed by extreme heat and pressure. It marked the borders of the North American continent until another mountain-building episode forced it up over newer, more easily eroded rocks.

This is glacier country, repeatedly covered and exposed as the ice sheets advanced and retreated during successive ice ages. That helps explain why the tops of mountains here are so barren and rocky and the valleys are so swampy and fertile: Soil was scraped off the top of the mountains and deposited in the valleys. Glacial "erratics"—large rocks left behind when the glaciers retreated—are common here, as are *roches moutonées*, or "sheepback" mountains, the south sides of which were shorn off by glacial action.

The Trail enters the Highlands area south of the Connecticut border in a swampy, hilly part of Dutchess County and runs generally north-east-to-southwest toward Putnam County. Historically, the area near the border was known as "the Oblong," a stretch of disputed New York–Connecticut boundary lands two miles wide and sixty miles long. The route descends through the Pawling Nature Reserve to the Harlem Valley, named for the New York and Harlem Railroad that ran south through it. From there, it crosses the "Great Swamp,"one of the largest wetlands in the state, and ascends and descends a series of ridges through old hillside farmland between the Harlem and Hudson valleys.

After crossing the Putnam County line on hills west of the Taconic Parkway and south of the Fishkill Plains, the A.T. enters Clarence Fahnestock State Park, a popular hiking, camping, and recreation area, the many side trails of which cross rocky hills that were once the site of nineteenth-century iron mines. It follows the ridges in the southern part of Hudson Highlands State Park and reaches the Hudson River Valley, where the river cuts between Bear Mountain and Anthony's Nose.

View of West Point from Anthony's Nose

Hudson River Valley—The lowest point on the entire Appalachian Trail (124 feet above sea level) is just south of the crossing of the Hudson River (which flows at sea level, 135 feet below the Bear Mountain Bridge). The Hudson River Valley is actually a fjord, or "drowned valley estuary," formed by the carving action of glaciers, then filled by the sea after the ice sheets melted and sea level rose. As such, it's the only fjord along the A.T. and one of the few on the east coast of North America. The water under the Bear Mountain Bridge is tidal and salty—and quite deep.

Historically, the Hudson served as a vital route to the American interior—first for native Americans, then for Dutch settlers of New York who first farmed the open areas north of the Highlands, then for early American industry. That made the narrow point between Bear Mountain and Anthony's Nose a key military choke-point, which explains the nearby facilities at West Point, Fort Montgomery, and Camp Smith. The hills on either side of the valley saw extensive Revolutionary War maneuvers, and the area was considered strategic as late as World War II, when the outbreak of hostilities resulted in the closing of the A.T. over Anthony's Nose.

After crossing the bridge, the Trail enters Bear Mountain State Park on the west side of the river and climbs back into the Highlands again. The park is a popular and convenient spot where day-trippers from New York City and other urban and suburban areas can climb a mountain, walk a trail, or picnic by a pond.

Harriman State Park and Sterling Forest—Hikers following the A.T. south from the Hudson River Valley into Orange County cross West Mountain and enter Harriman State Park, a vast woodland preserve within sight of the skyscrapers of Manhattan. The Highlands here were originally inhabited by the Delaware (Lenape) Indians until they were driven from their lands or wiped out by warfare and a variety of diseases introduced by European colonists. Like the mountains east of the Hudson, the region became a center for iron mining and forges from Revolutionary War times until the mid-1800s. Many sites of old forges and mines can still be found in the hills surrounding the Trail, including one located near what is now Lake Tiorati, dammed in the mid-1700s by an enterprising industrialist. The collapse of the region's mining economy after the Civil War sent land values plummeting, and large tracts were bought up by capitalists such as railroad magnate Edward Harriman. In the twentieth century, much of the Harriman property was sold or given to the state as parkland.

After scrambling through the claustrophobia-inducing crack of the Lemon Squeezer, a formation of ancient gneiss near the western boundary of the park, the southbound hiker crosses bridges over the Ramapo River and the busy New York State Thruway, then climbs onto a series of glacier-smoothed uplands near Mombasha Lake. This area, known as Sterling Forest, was also owned by the Harrimans and was slated for development until the late 1990s.

Before crossing into New Jersey, the route climbs the ridges of Bellvale Mountain above the lakeside houses and camps of Greenwood Lake and offers a few final glimpses of the New York City skyline. After crossing into New Jersey near Prospect Rock, it turns sharply to the northwest in Abram Hewitt State Forest and stops following the ridge, cutting across the grain of the mountains.

State Line Corridor—For about thirty miles, between Bearfort Mountain and High Point on Kittatinny Mountain, the A.T. in New Jersey parallels the state line, mostly in a narrow ribbon of land acquired in the 1980s by the state of New Jersey to protect the route. It passes through ridgetop state parks and the Wallkill National Wildlife Refuge. This preserve is the only national wildlife refuge along the entire A.T. Although the valleys are populated, hikers often encounter bears and other wildlife on the forested ridges, which seem much more remote than they really are. The ridges here are not particularly high, but they are often steep.

Historically, the ridges above the farms of the Vernon and Wallkill valleys were mined as part of the Highlands iron industry until after the Civil War, when the furnaces closed down. After industry's departure, the area's population in the early 1900s was actually lower than it was during the time of the American Revolution. It was rich farming country; today, the Trail in the valleys still passes across some farmland, as well as through suburban residential areas, wooded swamps, and floodplains. Water pollution has been a problem here.

The Lemon Squeezer

A new scenic boardwalk and suspension bridge, one of the biggest volunteer construction projects ever attempted on the A.T., crosses one of those floodplains at Pochuck Creek. This floodplain is the remains of a glacial lake that disappeared 10,000 years ago.

The Trail ascends and descends Pochuck Mountain, a last outcrop of the Highlands. The Wallkill Valley, which drains northward into the Hudson River, marks the end of the Highlands for the southbound hiker. From here south, the underlying rock begins changing from the older metamorphic rocks that typify New England, and the Trail turns toward what geologists call the Ridge and Valley Province—long, linear ridges and wide valleys that slant southwestward all the way to Tennessee. It's also the first time that a southbound A.T. hiker crosses the Great Valley of the Appalachians, the major geographic feature that includes the Cumberland, Shenandoah, and Tennessee valleys and runs from the Hudson all the way to Alabama. The Trail crosses the Great Valley several times between New York and Tennessee. Climbing out of the valley toward High Point State Park, hikers ascend Kittatinny Ridge, which they will follow into Pennsylvania.

Kittatinny Ridge—This long, narrow ridge runs like a wall near the northwestern boundary of New Jersey, and the Trail turns sharply southwestward again to follow it about forty miles in New Jersey. It gets its name from a native American word meaning "endless hills," and its stony, mostly level crest can seem endless compared to the ups and downs of the Highlands. Northeast of High Point State Park, where the ridge leads into New York State, it is called the Shawangunk Ridge. Southwest of the Delaware Water Gap, in Pennsylvania, it merges with another long ridge, Blue Mountain.

Geologists call the part of the Appalachians that the Trail follows south from here the Ridge and Valley Province, described by the U.S. Geological Survey as "alternating beds of hard and soft Paleozoic sedimentary rocks, folded like the wrinkles in a kicked floor rug." That pretty much sums it up. The folding took place when continents collided during the Paleozoic Era, about 500 million years ago. Ever since then, water has been eroding away the softer parts of the rock, forming the great valleys between the folds. The big wrinkle of Kittatinny Ridge has long been the wildest, least-settled part of New

Jersey and remains an area of Scout camps, weekend cottages, and wooded hills. An active bear population lives along the ridge. Water is scarce, and road crossings are few.

The entire route of the Trail along the ridge is in parkland or other protected areas. From High Point State Park, the Trail leads into Stokes State Forest and then the Delaware Water Gap National Recreation Area and descends to the Delaware Water Gap through Worthington State Forest.

Delaware Water Gap—The striking "water gap," where the Delaware River has carved its way through the ancient strata of the Appalachians, is a geologist's dream. Not only does it display dramatic rock formations, but it marks the southern boundary of Ice Age glaciers. Sunfish Pond, which the Trail skirts in Worthington State Forest, is the southernmost glacial pond along the Trail.

Historically, the Water Gap has also been a key route into the interior of the country, with the river leading from the port cities of Philadelphia and Trenton into the heart of Pennsylvania and New York State. The gap has long been a favorite resort destination and still serves as an important rail and highway route through the mountains and as the gateway to Pennsylvania's Poconos.

New York

New York is the Appalachian Trail's low point—and that's not a value judgment. The Hudson River flows at sea level where the Trail crosses it on Bear Mountain Bridge (pictured), between Bear Mountain and Anthony's Nose, where the river breaks through the Hudson Highlands. The A.T. dips down to 124 feet above sea level

there, its lowest elevation between Georgia and Maine. But New York has always been a key link in the Trail, and it's where the Trail began, in a sense—its first sections were built in Harriman and Bear Mountain state parks, and New York trailblazers were crucial to the founding of the Appalachian Trail Conference. The route through the Highlands of New York is a mix of rocky scrambles and walks along historic woodland ridges and glacial hills. Although hikers may find themselves within sight of the Manhattan skyline at a few overlooks, most of the route feels remote and dramatic, and takes them back to a time when these hills west of the city marked America's western frontier.

Conn. 341 (Kent) to Hoyt Road

11.5 MILES

This section begins in Connecticut and traverses the ridge of Schaghticoke and Algo mountains, crossing and recrossing the New York–Connecticut line through land that was an important area of native American settlements during colonial times. It is the only section of the entire A.T. to cross an Indian reservation. Highlights include views from Schaghticoke Mountain and a section that follows the gorge of the Housatonic River below Bulls Bridge. The Trail crosses Ten Mile River on a 120-foot bridge.

For Trail-management purposes, this section is designated as Connecticut Section Five rather than New York Section One, because most of it is maintained by the Connecticut Chapter of the Appalachian Mountain Club, even though the New York–New Jersey Trail Conference oversaw the relocation of part of the route in the 1990s.

Road Access—Both the northern and southern ends of this section are accessible by vehicle. Road access and parking are also available at Bulls Bridge Road (mile 7.4 below).

Maps—Refer to Map 1 with this guide, or to Map 5 in the *A.T. Guide to Massachusetts–Connecticut*. For area detail, refer to the following USGS 7½-minute topographic quadrangles: Kent, Connecticut, and Dover Plains, New York–Connecticut.

Shelters and Campsites—This section has two shelters (called "lean-tos" in Connecticut): Mt. Algo Lean-to, at mile 0.3 below, and Ten Mile River Lean-to, at mile 8.7 below. Two designated campsites are also available: Schaghticoke Mountain Campsite, at mile 3.2 below, and Ten Mile River Campsite, at mile 8.5 below. Campfires are not permitted in Connecticut.

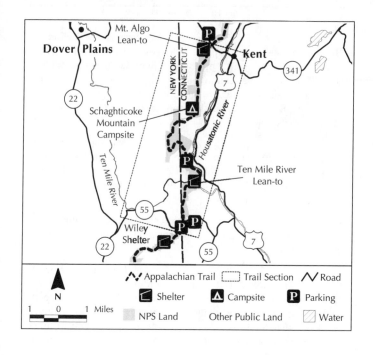

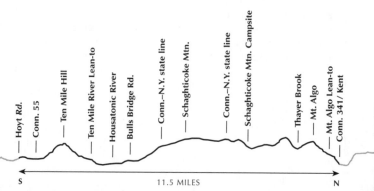

SECTION HIGHLIGHTS

Northern end of section →

The Trail crosses Conn. 341, 0.2 mile west of its intersection with Schaghticoke Road and 0.8 mile west of Kent, Connecticut. Parking is available at the intersection, but overnight parking is not recommended. Meals, groceries, lodging, and a post office (ZIP Code 06757) are available in Kent. Bus service to New York City and to Massachusetts is available.

Mt. Algo Lean-to →

Built in 1986; 200 feet from A.T. on side trail; accommodates six; privy; water available on trail from A.T. No fires permitted. Next shelter: north, 7.3 miles (Stewart Hollow Brook Lean-to); south, 8.4 miles (Ten Mile River Lean-to).

Schaghticoke Mountain Campsite →

A tent campsite, with privy and water available nearby. No fires are permitted.

Housatonic River →

Its name, *Housatonic,* comes from the Mohican Indian word for "place beyond the mountain." It was first explored by European settlers in 1614. Rising near Pittsfield, Massachusetts, it flows southward for 148 miles through Massachusetts and Connecticut to Long Island Sound. Historically, river power and river access made this an important farming and industrial area. Pollution has been a problem upstream, near Pittsfield, where PCB contamination at an EPA "Superfund" site is still being mitigated. Today, the water is relatively clean, but fishing is on a "catch-and-release" basis, and the river should not be used by hikers as a source of drinking water.

N-S

TRAIL DESCRIPTION

0.0	The **northern end of section** (elev. 350 ft.) is at Conn. 341. Southbound hikers ascend into woods. Northbound hikers cross Conn. 341 and descend toward Macedonia Brook. (See *Appalachian Trail Guide to Massachusetts–Connecticut*.)	**11.5**
0.3	Pass blue-blazed side trail, which leads west 200 feet to **Mt. Algo Lean-to** (elev. 650 ft.).	**11.2**
0.9	Cross height of land on Mt. Algo (elev. 1,190 ft.).	**10.6**
1.3	Cross Thayer Brook.	**10.2**
2.1	Reach crest of ridge on Schaghticoke Mountain.	**9.4**
2.4	Pass large rock, with views to south.	**9.1**
3.2	Near brook (reliable source of water) at bottom of Rattlesnake Den, a ravine with large hemlocks and jumbled boulders, a blue-blazed side trail leads west to **Schaghticoke Mountain Campsite**.	**8.3**
3.4	Reach an open ledge, with good views of the **Housatonic River**.	**8.1**
3.5	Trail descends into Dry Gulch, a rocky ravine on the east slope of Schaghticoke Mountain.	**8.0**

Housatonic River

S-N

Schaghticoke Indian Reservation →

The Trail briefly crosses this state-recognized reservation on a narrow corridor of land. The reservation, home of the Schaghticoke Tribal Nation, is the only native American property through which the A.T. passes, and its settled area consists of a handful of dwellings near the river. The tribe's original area was much larger, extending to and including the confluence of the Housatonic and Ten Mile rivers—one of the most important areas of native and Euroamerican heritage in northwestern Connecticut and the area's last Indian stronghold. Remnants of native American encampments nearby date back 4,000 years. The valley of the Ten Mile River was the natural highway to the Housatonic River Valley, and Indians entering there spread throughout Connecticut. Early accounts of the area mention that the floodplain was covered with Indian cornfields and wigwams. The Kent corridor is a highly sensitive archaeological area. In 1730, one hundred Indian families lived here; two decades later, only eighteen remained; today, about half a dozen families live in the area.

Schaghticoke Road →

Leads north along the Housatonic River, through the Indian reservation and past Kent School, to the town of Kent, Connecticut.

Bulls Bridge Road →

To west becomes Dogtail Corners Road in New York, once a direct route between Hartford, Connecticut, and Poughkeepsie, New York. Now leads west, by way of Dogtail Corners, to the New York communities of Webatuck and Wingdale and east, by way of Bulls Bridge (0.5 mile), to U.S. 7 and the Connecticut community of South Kent. Parking is available near the covered bridge (see mile 7.9 below). Food and groceries are available 0.6 mile east of the Trail at Bulls Bridge.

N-S

| TRAIL DESCRIPTION |

3.8 Reach Indian Rocks (elev. 1,330 ft.), a fine outlook to the east near **Schaghticoke Indian Reservation**, with winter views of the river valley and U.S. 7 below. **7.7**

4.1 Trail crosses a stream. **7.4**

4.2 Pass a sign marking the New York–Connecticut boundary on the west side of the Trail. **7.3**

4.5 Trail turns sharply. **7.0**

5.1 Pass two views to west over Ellis Pond. **6.4**

5.4 Trail passes just west of the summit of Schaghticoke Mountain (elev. 1,331 ft.). Between here and Schaghticoke Road, southbound hikers descend on numerous switchbacks, crossing the New York–Connecticut boundary (unmarked) again. **6.1**

5.6 Pass a viewpoint to the southwest from open rocks, near a sharp turn in the Trail. **5.9**

6.1 Pass an old stone fireplace to the west, near a gully, above switchbacks. **5.4**

6.4 The Trail follows stone steps above a steep, switchbacked section. **5.1**

6.8 Cross a stream near a hemlock grove. **4.7**

7.1 The Trail intersects with paved **Schaghticoke Road** (elev. 360 ft.) at the foot of Schaghticoke Mountain. Southbound hikers turn right and follow road. Northbound hikers leave road and enter woods at left, then immediately turn right and begin to parallel stream and road, ascending Schaghticoke Mountain *via* switchbacks. **4.4**

7.4 Intersection of **Schaghticoke Road** and **Bulls Bridge Road**. Southbound hikers cross road and ascend rise. Northbound hikers follow Schaghticoke Road. **4.1**

S-N

Bulls Bridge →

An old farm road leads from the A.T. to a parking area on Bulls Bridge Road. The bridge is one of two remaining covered bridges in Connecticut that still permit traffic. It was named after an early settler who had an inn (near the present location of the Bulls Bridge Inn) that often catered to George Washington, among others. Washington's horse is said to have fallen off or through the bridge here. Across the road from the parking lot is a dam, built in 1902, that is worth a visit when the river is running high. Just below the gorge on the east side of the river are the remains of an old blast furnace. In the eighteenth century, Kent was second to Salisbury, Connecticut, as a source of high-quality iron ore.

Ned Anderson Memorial Bridge →

The Trail crosses the Ten Mile River on this bridge, built in 1983. The steel-reinforced span was prefabricated, shipped by truck, and installed with a crane. Ned Anderson was a farmer from Sherman who designed, built, and, for 20 years, maintained the original Trail in Connecticut. It was then a project of the Connecticut Forest and Park Association (1929-1949). Interestingly enough, the Trail did not enter the town of Sherman until 1984, because the only way to cross the Ten Mile River until then was by a highway bridge in New York.

Ten Mile River Camping Area →

A camping area is in the field south of the bridge, as are a water pump and privy. No fires are allowed. Group camping is north of the bridge.

N-S

TRAIL DESCRIPTION

Bulls Bridge

7.9 Trail turns 90 degrees at intersection with old farm road (leads compass-north to parking area for **Bulls Bridge**). Southbound hikers turn right along west bank of Housatonic River on the old road and then a scenic riverside footpath. Northbound hikers turn left, leaving the farm road, and ascend rise. **3.6**

8.4 Pass through a gap in a stone wall near a small brook. Southbound hikers pass under powerlines, with view of Ten Mile Hill to the south. Northbound hikers follow scenic riverbank trail toward **Bulls Bridge**. **3.1**

8.5 Cross Ten Mile River on **Ned Anderson Memorial Bridge**. Pass **Ten Mile River Camping Area** in a field south of the bridge. A side trail leads to a **group camping area** at the north end of bridge. Southbound hikers follow the south bank of Ten Mile River. Northbound hikers follow west bank of Housatonic River. **3.0**

S-N

Ten Mile River Lean-to →

Built in 1996, this shelter accommodates six. A privy is nearby. Water is available 0.1 mile north along the A.T. at a water pump. No campfires are permitted. Next shelter: north, 8.4 miles (Mt. Algo Lean-to); south, 4.0 miles (Wiley Shelter).

Herrick Trail →

Leads around Ten Mile Hill, 1.0 mile, to view of Housatonic River.

Conn. 55 →

Leads west 4.0 miles to the New York communities of Webatuck and Wingdale and east to the Housatonic River and U.S. 7. No parking at road crossing, but a large parking area is just east of the Connecticut–New York line, 0.2 mile west of the Trail crossing of Conn. 55. This parking area is connected by a short side trail to the A.T., 0.3 mile from the southern end of the section.

Southern end of section →

Parking for several cars is available near the Trail crossing. No public transportation is available at the Trailhead, but a Metro-North Railroad station is 4.3 miles from the Trail, south of Wingdale, New York. Meals are available on N.Y. 55 at a café 1.5 miles west of Hoyt Road (follow Hoyt Road compass-north 0.3 mile to N.Y. 55, then west); more restaurants and a post office (ZIP Code 12594) are available in Wingdale, 3.3 miles west of the Trail crossing of Hoyt Road. No accommodations are available at the southern end of the section.

N-S	TRAIL DESCRIPTION	
8.7	Blue-blazed side trail leads east 0.1 mile to **Ten Mile River Lean-to.**	2.8
9.0	Cross a dirt road.	2.5
9.2	Pass an intermittent spring to the west of the Trail, which follows several old woods roads through this section.	2.3
9.6	Blue-blazed **Herrick Trail** intersects on east side of the A.T.	1.9
9.7	Reach the top of Ten Mile Hill (elev. 1,000 ft.), with limited views.	1.8
10.8	Cross paved **Conn. 55**. Southbound hikers follow edge of field.	0.7
11.0	Cross brook, a reliable water source.	0.5
11.2	Near the border of woods and field, a side trail to the west leads to a large parking area on **Conn. 55** for the southern end of section.	0.3
11.5	The **southern end of section** is where the Trail intersects with Hoyt Road (elev. 420 ft.) at the Connecticut–New York state line. Southbound hikers turn right on road (see New York Section Two). Northbound hikers enter a small field across road.	0.0

S-N

Hoyt Road to N.Y. 22 (Pawling)

7.1 MILES

The Trail here passes through second-growth woodlands that range from scrubby to mature, including several groves of hemlocks and stands of mixed hardwoods along the Hammersly Ridge. Bog bridges lead across several marshy, high-elevation swamps in an area that is an important watershed for one of the state's largest freshwater wetlands. You may glimpse the rolling countryside of southern Dutchess County. Evidence of the past can be observed in the crumbling stone walls, foundations, dams, and traces of abandoned orchards, fields, and roads. This area was farmed extensively through the eighteenth century, but much of the land has long since reverted to forest. Many marked trails in the Pawling Nature Reserve (maintained by volunteers and friends of the reserve) intersect with the A.T. Elevation at Hoyt Road is 420 feet, and, at N.Y. 22, it is 450 feet. The highest point is on the Hammersly Ridge, with an elevation of 1,053 feet.

Road Approaches—Both ends are accessible by vehicle. Road access is also available at Duell Hollow Road, mile 1.0 below.

Maps—For route navigation, refer to Map 1 with this guide. For area detail, refer to the following USGS 7½-minute topographic quadrangles: Dover Plains, New York-Connecticut; Pawling, New York-Connecticut. A map of Pawling Nature Reserve is available from the Lower Hudson Chapter of The Nature Conservancy.

Shelters and Campsites—This section has one shelter, Wiley Shelter (mile 1.2 below). Camping is not permitted elsewhere. Campfires are permitted only in fireplaces at designated shelters or campsites.

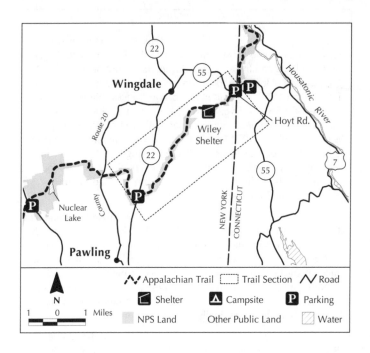

Appalachian Trail · Trail Section · Road
Shelter · Campsite · P Parking
N
1 0 1 Miles
NPS Land · Other Public Land · Water

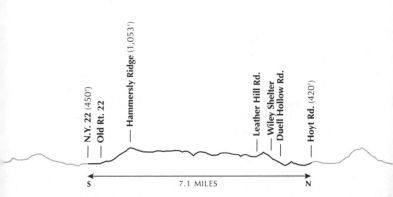

S · 7.1 MILES · N

Northern end of section →

Parking is available for several cars near the Trail crossing. In addition, a large parking area is on Conn. 55 (a continuation of N.Y. 55), just east of the New York–Connecticut line, 0.3 mile east of the intersection of N.Y. 55 with Hoyt Road and accessible *via* trail (see Connecticut Section Five, above). Meals are available at a café on N.Y. 55, 1.5 miles west of Hoyt Road (follow Hoyt Road compass-north 0.3 mile to N.Y. 55, then west); more restaurants and a post office (ZIP Code 12594) are available in Wingdale, N.Y., 3.3 miles west of the Trail crossing of Hoyt Road. No public transportation is available at the Trailhead, but a Metro-North Railroad station is 4.3 miles from the Trail, south of Wingdale.

Duell Hollow Road →

Leads west 0.7 mile to N.Y. 55. Limited parking is available just south of the Trail crossing, near an old cemetery. This two-mile-wide part of New York was known as "The Oblong" and extended about 60 miles along the Connecticut border. The border between the colonies of New York and Connecticut was contested because of inexact surveys during the seventeenth and eighteenth centuries; it remained disputed until the states finally settled things in 1880.

Wiley Shelter →

Built in 1940, with assistance from William O. Wiley of the Tramp and Trail Club of New York, on property that was once Boy Scout Camp Siwanoy; accommodates 6; water available from pump on Trail 0.1 mile north. Next shelter: north, 4.0 miles (Ten Mile River Lean-to); south, 9.0 miles (Telephone Pioneers Shelter).

Gate of Heaven →

The wrought-iron gate leads to a small cemetery on the grounds of the former Harlem Valley state mental hospital, which is downhill from the site, to the west. Only a handful of graves, from the mid-twentieth century, are marked.

N-S

TRAIL DESCRIPTION

N-S		S-N
0.0	Hoyt Road, at the **northern end of section**. Southbound hikers proceed north on Hoyt Road, then turn left and enter woods. Northbound hikers turn left off the road and cross the end of a small field.	7.1
0.2	Trail briefly follows old woods road between an overgrown field and an open field.	6.9
0.7	Cross wooden bridge over Duell Hollow Brook.	6.4
1.0	Cross paved **Duell Hollow Road**, at foot of hill.	6.1
1.1	Pass pump, a water source.	6.0
1.2	A.T. crosses a stone wall and passes in front of **Wiley Shelter**.	5.9
1.3	Cross dirt logging road.	5.8
1.6	Cross dirt Leather Hill Road.	5.5
1.7	Pass through gap in stone wall, north of stream crossing.	5.4
1.9	Trail follows old woods road.	5.2
2.1	Cross cleared strip of land (telephone cable) to north of stone wall.	5.0
2.4	Pass **Gate of Heaven** Cemetery on dirt road. Northbound hikers enter woods at left. Southbound hikers follow dirt road.	4.7
2.6	Southbound hikers turn right, into woods, and cross gravel road. Northbound hikers turn left on dirt road.	4.5
3.0	Pass through gap in stone wall.	4.1
3.1	Cross a stream on rocks.	4.0
3.3	Cross a stream on logs.	3.8

S-N

Pawling Nature Reserve →

Covering 1,071 acres, this Nature Conservancy reserve includes several trails but no public facilities. Stretching along Hammersly Ridge, it includes steep ravines shadowed by "hemlock cathedrals," oak forests, and red maple–hardwood swamps, all in close proximity. The land was worked extensively from colonial times through the nineteenth century, with some hayfields harvested as late as the 1970s. A map of Pawling Nature Reserve is available from the Lower Hudson Chapter of The Nature Conservancy, 41 South Moger Avenue, Mt. Kisco, NY 10549, (914) 244-3271.

Yellow Trail →

Leads east 0.7 mile to parking area at north entrance of Pawling Nature Reserve on Quaker Lake Road (Duell Hollow Road).

Red Trail →

Leads east 1.5 miles to main entrance and parking area of Pawling Nature Reserve on Quaker Lake Road (Duell Hollow Road); its route parallels or coincides with the A.T. for 0.9 mile south of the intersection.

Green Trail →

Leads west 1.0 mile to Sprague Road and can be used to access the Harlem Valley-Wingdale railroad station on N.Y. 22, a mile south of Wingdale, New York. To reach the A.T. from this station, cross U.S. 22 at the traffic light and proceed for 0.2 mile on Wheeler Road, turn right onto Hutchinson Avenue and continue for 0.6 mile, then turn left onto Sprague Road and proceed for 0.2 mile to the entrance of the Pawling Nature Reserve, and the trailhead. Meals, lodging, and a limited selection of groceries may be obtained from establishments located on N.Y. 22 near the station.

Swamp →

Botanists call these red maple–hardwood swamps "palustrine wetlands" (from the Latin word "palus," or marsh), by which they mean shallow freshwater swamps; these were formed by retreating glaciers after the last Ice Age.

N-S	TRAIL DESCRIPTION	
3.5	Northern boundary of **Pawling Nature Reserve**.	3.6
3.6	**Yellow Trail** intersects on east side of A.T.	3.5
4.4	Cross a swampy area on logs.	2.7
4.5	Pass intersections of Red and Green trails. **Red Trail** intersects on the east side of A.T., where the Trail turns sharply. **Green Trail** intersects on the west side, 125 feet farther south.	2.6
4.7	Cross a long section of puncheon over a swampy area.	2.4
4.9	Cross a stream to north of **Yellow Trail** intersection.	2.2
5.2	Cross a stream.	1.9
5.3	Pass a **swamp** to west of Trail.	1.8
5.4	Pass the terminus of **Red Trail**.	1.7
5.6	Cross height of land at Hammersly Ridge (elev. 1,053 ft.).	1.5
6.2	Cross a brook (elev. 670 ft.).	0.9

SECTION HIGHLIGHTS

Blue-blazed trail →

Former A.T. route leads 0.3 mile west to Hurds Corners Road.

Water tower →

Constructed about 1920 by a local dairy, the tower supplied water during periods of peak demand. It fell into disrepair but was restored in 1989 by the Hurds Corner Civic Association, with assistance from the New York–New Jersey Trail Conference and the Appalachian Trail Conference.

Southern end of section →

A designated parking area is just north of the Trail crossing. Rail service to New York City (Grand Central Terminal) *via* the Metro-North Railroad is available at Pawling, 2.4 miles south. On weekends and holidays, Metro-North provides rail service at the Appalachian Trail station at the Trail crossing. Limited bus service is available to Pawling and Poughkeepsie, *via* the Dutchess County Loop Bus System. A grocery store is located on N.Y. 22, 0.6 mile south of the Trail crossing, and groceries, meals, a post office (ZIP Code 12564), a coin laundry, and other supplies and services are available in Pawling. A motel on N.Y. 22 is located 2.6 miles north of the Trail crossing and 0.6 mile south of the Harlem Valley-Wingdale railroad station.

N-S

TRAIL DESCRIPTION

6.3 Reach junction (please sign register) with **blue-blazed trail** on west side of A.T., at a sharp turn, near southern boundary of **Pawling Nature Reserve**. **0.8**

6.6 Cross stile over electrified fence, north of open field. **0.5**

6.7 Cross stream on wooden bridge, north of stile over fence, with views over field to west of a **water tower**. **0.4**

6.9 Cross paved Hurds Corners Road (Old Route 22) with fences on either side of road. The road leads leads west to N.Y. 22, south of Wingdale. **0.2**

7.1 The **southern end of section** is at N.Y. 22, just east (compass-north) of the Appalachian Trail rail station of the Metro-North Railroad. Southbound hikers continue across road and proceed compass-south on N.Y. 22. Northbound hikers follow posts along field, proceeding compass-east (New York Section Three below). **0.0**

S-N

N.Y. 22 (Pawling) to N.Y. 55 (Poughquag)

7.4 MILES

This section of Trail crosses the Harlem Valley, named for the New York and Harlem Railroad that connected upstate New York with Manhattan Island. The route skirts the Great Swamp, the second-largest freshwater wetland in the state and an important ecological area. The northern part climbs Corbin Hill, proceeds through open fields, and then steeply climbs West Mountain to a beautiful viewpoint over the countryside to the east. The southern part of the section runs alongside scenic Nuclear Lake, formerly the site of a nuclear testing facility but now cleaned and open for unrestricted use. A 1998 reroute takes the Trail along the shore of the lake, thus enabling hikers to experience the beauty of this scenic area.

Road Approaches—Both the northern and southern ends of this section are accessible by vehicle. Road access is also available at County 20 (West Dover Road), which crosses the A.T. at mile 2.4 below.

Maps—For route navigation, refer to Map 1 with this guide. For area detail, refer to the following USGS 7½-minute topographic quadrangles: Pawling, New York-Connecticut; Poughquag, New York.

Shelters and Campsites—This section has one shelter, Telephone Pioneers Shelter (mile 3.1 below). One public campground, Edward R. Murrow Memorial Park (mile 2.4 below), is 3.1 miles from the Trail. Otherwise, no camping is permitted in the section. Campfires are permitted only at fireplaces at designated shelters or campsites.

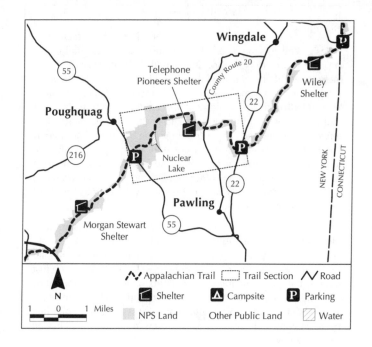

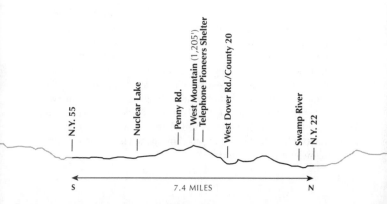

Northern end of section →

A designated parking area is located just north of the Trail crossing. Rail service to New York City (Grand Central Terminal) *via* the Metro-North Railroad is available at Pawling (also accessible from West Dover Road, mile 2.4 below). On weekends and holidays, Metro-North provides limited rail service at the Appalachian Trail station, just west of the northern end of the section. Limited bus service to Pawling and Poughkeepsie, *via* the Dutchess County Loop Bus System, is available. A grocery store is on N.Y. 22, 0.6 mile south of the Trail crossing. Groceries, meals, a post office (ZIP Code 12564), a coin laundry, and other supplies and services are available in Pawling. A motel on N.Y. 22 is 2.6 miles west (compass-north) of the northern end of the section.

Appalachian Trail station →

Metro-North Railroad's Appalachian Trail station (trains stop weekends and holidays only) is at the Trail crossing; the nearest regular stop is in Pawling. These tracks along the Harlem Valley were first built by the New York and Harlem Railroad, which gave the valley its name. The railroad dates back to 1831 and was later part of the Vanderbilt railroad empire. At the time, it was a vital transport link between New York City and upstate New York when the Hudson River froze over.

Swamp River →

This lazy watercourse is at the heart of the Great Swamp, the second-largest freshwater wetland in the state of New York. The swamp extends more than 20 miles across 4,800 acres in Putnam and Dutchess counties along N.Y. 22 and is home to at least nine rare plant and animal species, as well as a dazzling variety of other wildlife and plants. In addition to absorbing storm runoff, the wetland filters drinking water for millions of people in Dutchess and Westchester counties and New York City. The swamp is a popular destination for canoeing, fishing and birding, but development along the highway is encroaching on it.

N-S

TRAIL DESCRIPTION

Appalachian Trail station

0.0	The **northern end of section** is at N.Y. 22. Southbound hikers proceed compass-south on N.Y. 22. Northbound hikers follow posts along field, proceeding compass-east (New York Section Two above).	**7.4**
0.1	A dirt road intersects on the west side of N.Y. 22. Southbound hikers follow dirt road, cross railroad tracks at **Appalachian Trail station**, go around gate, and follow road alongside field. Northbound hikers follow N.Y. 22 north.	**7.3**
0.4	Cross **Swamp River** (elev. 415 ft.) at the foot of Corbin Hill. Southbound hikers cross a marshy area on puncheon, then cross a wooden bridge, turn right, and begin steady ascent of Corbin Hill (elev. 760 ft.). Northbound hikers cross the river and puncheon, then follow a dirt road alongside a field.	**7.0**
0.9	Pass through gap in a stone wall.	**6.5**

S-N

SECTION HIGHLIGHTS

Dover Oak →

With a girth of nearly 20 feet, it is probably the largest oak tree along the Appalachian Trail, rivaled only by the Keffer Oak in Sinking Creek Valley, Virginia. Drinking water is available to hikers from a spigot in the driveway of a gray house just off the A.T., on the south side of West Dover Road.

County 20 (West Dover Road) →

Leads south 2.9 miles to the center of Pawling, N.Y. (after 2.1 miles, at intersection with Corbin Road and Lakeside Drive, the road name changes to Charles Colman Boulevard). Camping is available at Edward R. Murrow Memorial Park in Pawling (named in memory of the pioneer of American broadcast journalism, a resident of Pawling at the time of his death in 1965), operated by Pawling Recreation Department, at junction of Lakeside Drive and Old N.Y. 55, 3.1 miles from the Trail crossing. Open year-round, with a nominal fee charged. Swimming, cold showers, and snack bar available (Memorial Day to Labor Day); picnic shelters with fireplaces also available. Groceries, meals, a post office (ZIP Code 12564), a coin laundry, and other supplies and services are available in Pawling. The post office is on Broad Street, just west of the center of town. A supermarket (open seven days a week) is on East Main Street, 0.2 mile east of the intersection of Charles Colman Boulevard and East Main Street.

Telephone Pioneers Shelter →

Built in 1988 with assistance from the White Plains Council of the Telephone Pioneers of America; accommodates 6; water from un-reliable stream crossed by side trail to shelter; privy 200 feet from shelter on side trail. Next shelter: north, 9.0 miles (Wiley Shelter); south, 7.6 miles (Morgan Stewart Memorial Shelter). When stream is dry, water is available from house near Dover Oak (see mile 2.4).

N-S

| | TRAIL DESCRIPTION | |

1.1	Pass through large gap in a stone wall.	6.3
1.5	Trail levels off at the top of hill.	5.9
1.6	Trail follows the edge of a field next to woods. Southbound hikers follow posts across field. Northbound hikers enter woods.	5.8
1.9	Skirt edge of field on puncheon and bridges in marshy area. *Caution: The fence around the field may be electrified.*	5.5
2.4	Pass the **Dover Oak**, a huge white oak next to the Trail, between **County 20 (West Dover Road)** and stone steps.	5.0
2.5	Follow posts through open fields.	4.9
2.7	Cross stream (elev. 520 ft.) at foot of steep slope of West Mountain.	4.7
3.1	Side trail leads 0.1 mile east to **Telephone Pioneers Shelter**.	4.3
3.3	A side trail leads 100 feet west to a rocky ledge with views over farmlands below.	4.1
3.4	Reach height of land (elev. 1,205 ft.) on West Mountain, with views to compass-north of Dutchess County.	4.0
3.8	Pass swamp to right of Trail.	3.6
3.9	Cross Penny Road (dirt, not passable by car).	3.5
4.1	At a low point between hills, cross brook and swampy area on puncheon.	3.3
4.5	Pass through gap in stone wall above a steep slope.	2.9

S-N

SECTION HIGHLIGHTS

Beekman Uplands Trail →

Former A.T. route, which bypassed Nuclear Lake before the site was cleaned up. The original land grant (royal patent) for the region was given to Col. Henry Beekman in 1697 and was the second largest patent in present-day Dutchess County. Towns in the patent included Beekman, Dover, LaGrange, Pawling, and Union Vale.

Nuclear Lake Loop →

Leads 1.1 miles along east shore of the lake. When combined with the A.T., a 1.9-mile loop around the lake is possible. The loop trail follows the shoreline, crossing streams, swamps, and the dam access road.

Nuclear Lake →

A nuclear fuels-processing research facility operated here until 1972. Subsequently, the National Park Service acquired the land for the Trail corridor. At first, there were fears that the lake was contaminated. The buildings were razed, and the area was tested extensively and given a clean bill of health. The site is suitable for unrestricted use. The clearing to the east is the site of a former lodge. The sound of gunshots from a gun club east of the Trail may be noticeable in the vicinity of the lake.

Southern end of section →

About 5.0 miles northeast of the intersection of N.Y. 55 and N.Y. 22, and 1.5 miles southeast of the intersection of N.Y. 55 with N.Y. 216. A designated parking area is located 0.1 mile west of the Trail crossing. Limited bus service to Pawling and Poughkeepsie is available. A large supermarket (open seven days a week) is on N.Y. 55, 3.6 miles northwest of the Trail crossing. A limited selection of groceries and light meals are available at a store at N.Y. 216. Meals and a post office (ZIP Code 12570) are available in Poughquag, on N.Y. 55, 3.1 miles west of the end of the section. A motel is also located on N.Y. 55, 2.6 miles west of the southern end of the section.

N-S

TRAIL DESCRIPTION

4.9 Blue-blazed **Beekman Uplands Trail** intersects on the west side of the A.T. (rejoins A.T. at mile 7.1 below). **2.5**

5.0 Cross an intermittent stream. **2.4**

5.3 Yellow-blazed **Nuclear Lake Loop** intersects on east side of A.T. where the Trail crosses several stone walls. There is much evidence of beaver activity in the area. **2.1**

5.8 Trail follows an old road along the western shore of **Nuclear Lake**. **1.6**

6.1 Yellow-blazed **Nuclear Lake Loop** intersects on the west side of the Trail. Southbound hikers leave the road and lake area, passing through a mountain-laurel thicket. Northbound hikers follow the road along the west shore of lake. **1.3**

6.2 Cross stream, the outlet of Nuclear Lake (with a small waterfall a short distance upstream), in rocky section. **1.2**

6.4 Pass through a small hemlock grove. **1.0**

6.6 Cross a small stream. **0.8**

7.1 Blue-blazed **Beekman Uplands Trail** intersects on the west side of the A.T. (rejoins A.T. at mile 4.9 above). **0.3**

7.2 Blue-blazed side trail to west leads to parking area on N.Y. 55. **0.2**

7.4 Reach the **southern end of section** at paved N.Y. 55. Southbound hikers cross the road and reenter woods (see New York Section Four, below). Northbound hikers follow the A.T. under powerlines. **0.0**

S-N

N.Y. 55 (Poughquag) to N.Y. 52 (Stormville)

7.2 MILES

This section goes over Depot Hill, south of Poughquag, New York. Though not particularly high (the highest point in the section is the summit of Mt. Egbert on Depot Hill, which is 1,329 feet), the route requires a good bit of scrambling up and down ravines and knolls atop the ridge. That is rewarded by several beautiful views from rock ledges of the "plains" of Dutchess County and the surrounding Hudson Highlands. Except for a few short stretches along roads, the Trail passes mostly through woods. It runs near the site of a former community of freed slaves known as "Freemanville." The elevation at the northern end of the section is about 470 feet, and, at the southern end, it is about 850 feet.

Road Approaches—Both the northern and southern ends of this section are accessible by vehicle. Road access is also available at Depot Hill Road (mile 2.2 below), Grape Hollow Road, and Mountain Top Road at the I-84 overpass (mile 5.8 below). Parking is available at or near those locations.

Maps—For route navigation, refer to Map 1 with this guide. For area detail, refer to the following USGS 7½-minute topographic quadrangle: Poughquag, New York.

Shelters and Campsites—This section has one shelter: Morgan Stewart Memorial Shelter (mile 3.3 below). No camping is permitted elsewhere in the section.

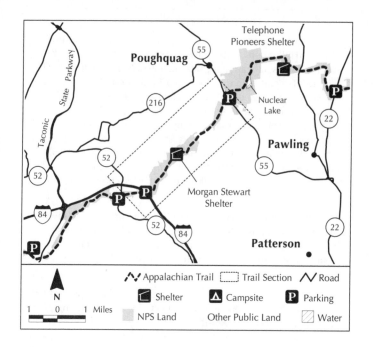

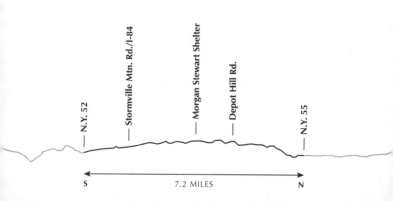

Northern end of section →

About 5.0 miles northeast of the intersection of N.Y. 55 and N.Y. 22, and 1.5 miles southeast of the intersection of N.Y. 55 with N.Y. 216. A designated parking area is located 0.1 mile west of the Trail crossing. Limited bus service to Pawling and Poughkeepsie is available. A large supermarket (open seven days a week) is on N.Y. 55, 3.6 miles northwest of the Trail crossing. A limited selection of groceries and light meals are available at a store at N.Y. 216. Meals and a post office (ZIP Code 12570) are available in Poughquag, on N.Y. 55, 3.1 miles west of the end of the section. A motel is also located on N.Y. 55, 2.6 miles west of the northern end of the section.

Old N.Y. 55 →

The nineteenth-century Beekman-to-Pawling Turnpike over Pawling Mountain was a privately owned toll road from 1824 to 1906 and an important route until N.Y. 55 was relocated. An eighteenth-century stone house, formerly the Stonehouse/West Pawling post office, is near here.

Railroad tracks →

Originally the New York and New England Railroad, serving as an approach to the Poughkeepsie Railroad Bridge, completed in 1888. The line eventually became part of the New York, New Haven, and Hartford Railroad. It was never a significant passenger line, but served as a key link in an important freight route. It became less significant after the New Haven Railroad was merged into the Penn Central in the late 1960s. The bridge was damaged by fire in 1974, and the rail line was sold to the Metro-North Railroad. Today, it is used for non-revenue equipment moves and occasional passenger excursions. Long-range plans call for commuter service to New York City on this route.

N-S

TRAIL DESCRIPTION

0.0 The **northern end of section** is at N.Y. 55. Southbound hikers cross road and reenter woods. Northbound hikers follow A.T. under powerlines (see New York Section Three, above). **7.2**

0.3 Reach paved road (**Old N.Y. 55**). Southbound hikers descend wooden steps and cross muddy area on rocks. **6.9**

0.4 Cross **railroad tracks**. Southbound hikers descend from embankment, cross a small brook, and soon begin ascending Depot Hill. Northbound hikers cross wooden bridge over Whaley Lake Stream (elev. 670 ft.). **6.8**

0.9 Pass a balanced rock to the east. **6.3**

1.6 Cross the northern boundary of state forest land, Depot Hill Multiple Use Area (marked by yellow blazes on trees). **5.6**

1.8 Cross height of land (elev. 1,265 ft.). **5.4**

Metro-North Railroad

S-N

Depot Hill Road →

Leads west, about five miles, to Poughquag, N.Y. At the foot of Depot Hill near where the road crosses the old NY&NE tracks, turn-of-the-century maps show a rail depot, apparently where the hill's name comes from. One nineteenth-century history of Dutchess County locates Freemanville, a community built around the property of freed slave Charles Freeman, near here.

Dutchess County →

Named not for its original Dutch settlers, but rather an antique spelling of "Duchess," after Mary, Duchess of York, second wife of James, Duke of York (later King James II of England), after whom New York was named in 1674. Dutch immigrants displaced native Americans there in the 1620s. The first settlements along the Hudson were predominantly Dutch and French Protestants, while settlers from New England inhabited the eastern part of the county. A notable settlement of Quakers settled the hills east of the Trail. During the Revolutionary War, the town of Pawling was the site of a great deal of conflict, and George Washington established a temporary headquarters there.

Morgan Stewart Memorial Shelter →

Built in 1984 by local volunteers; accommodates 6; water from dependable well on 400-foot side trail leading downhill from front of shelter; privy located 200 feet from shelter on side trail. Hikers should treat the well water. Next shelter: north 7.6 miles (Telephone Pioneers Shelter); south 9.0 miles (RPH Shelter).

Green Haven prison →

A maximum-security prison that serves as home to New York's death row, formerly located at Sing Sing prison. For more than a decade, it was home to the state's electric chair. It was the last of the state's "big house" prisons to be constructed, opening after World War II, and today houses more that 2,000 inmates, most of whom have committed violent offenses and sixty percent of whom are serving life sentences.

N-S	TRAIL DESCRIPTION	
1.9	Follow a narrow passage between rocks near a highland swamp.	**5.3**
2.2	Near a radio tower, cross unpaved **Depot Hill Road**, southern boundary of state forest land, Depot Hill Multiple Use Area (marked by yellow blazes on trees).	**5.0**
2.7	Pass seasonal pond to the east of the Trail and just north and above a narrow ravine below Mt. Egbert, with rock steps.	**4.5**
3.0	Reach rock ledge with good views to north of **Dutchess County**.	**4.2**
3.3	Side trail on left leads 75 feet to **Morgan Stewart Memorial Shelter**.	**3.9**
3.4	Summit of Mt. Egbert (elev. 1,329 ft.), with a U.S. Coast and Geodetic Survey marker affixed to a rock. Visible about a mile to the west (compass-north) is New York's **Green Haven prison**.	**3.8**
3.6	Reach ridgecrest ledge with good views to west and south, above steep 200-foot slope.	**3.6**
3.7	Pass an old stone foundation to west.	**3.5**
3.9	Cross a brook, with steep ascents on both sides.	**3.3**
4.3	Pass through a cleft in a rock at top of a knoll.	**2.9**
5.5	Cross a hollow, with a swampy area to the east.	**1.7**

SECTION HIGHLIGHTS

Grape Hollow Road →
Leads west about two miles to N.Y. 52. Parking available along the road west of the A.T.

Interstate 84 overpass →
I-84 runs 234 miles from Scranton, Pennsylvania, to Sturbridge, Massachusetts by way of Hartford, Connecticut.

Shawangunk and Catskill mountains →
The Catskills, northwest of the A.T. and west of the Hudson River near Kingston, New York, are one of New York's most scenic areas, and their streams and lakes provide drinking water for New York City. The Shawangunks, closer to the A.T., run along the west side of the Great Valley of the Appalachians, west of the Hudson near New Paltz.

Southern end of section →
On N.Y. 52, 0.4 mile west (compass-north) of the intersection of N.Y. 52 with Leetown Road and 2.2 miles east (compass-south) of Stormville (*via* Old N.Y. 52). A designated parking area is located just north of the Trail crossing. Groceries and sandwiches are available at a store (open seven days a week) 0.5 mile east (compass-south) of the Trail crossing, on Leetown Road. Groceries and light meals are also available at a store (open seven days a week) 2.0 miles east (compass-south) of the Trail crossing on N.Y. 52. Stormville has a post office (ZIP Code 12582) and a meat market that carries a limited selection of groceries (closed Mondays), 2.2 miles west (compass-north) of the Trail crossing (proceed north on N.Y. 52 for 1.7 miles, then turn right onto Old N.Y. 52, and continue for 0.5 mile). Another store with a limited supply of groceries (open seven days a week) and a public telephone is 0.2 mile farther north, at the intersection of Old N.Y. 52 and N.Y. 216. No public transportation is available.

N-S

TRAIL DESCRIPTION

5.8 Cross paved **Grape Hollow Road**, at foot of Depot Hill. Southbound hikers continue straight ahead on Mountain Top Road and cross **Interstate 84** on overpass. Northbound hikers cross guardrail and descend stone steps from road embankment. **1.4**

6.0 Intersection of paved Stormville Mountain Road with Mountain Top Road. Southbound hikers follow Stormville Mountain Road to right. Northbound hikers follow Mountain Top Road toward **Interstate 84 overpass**. **1.2**

6.2 A.T. intersects with Stormville Mountain Road near dead-end of road. Southbound hikers turn left and ascend on footpath into woods. Northbound hikers follow road to right. **1.0**

6.4 Cross an overgrown field, with portions cleared as part of an open-areas management project for improved views and natural diversity. There are wide views of the **Shawangunk and Catskill mountains** to the north and northwest. **0.8**

6.6 Cross a stone wall above and north of a small stream crossing. **0.6**

6.7 Pass through a gap in an old stone wall. **0.5**

7.1 A.T. intersects with a blue-blazed trail to a parking area on N.Y. 52. Southbound hikers turn left, off old woods road. Northbound hikers follow A.T. along old woods road. **0.1**

7.2 A.T. intersects with N.Y. 52. Southbound hikers cross the highway, turn left, and follow it east for 125 feet to **southern end of section**. Northbound hikers cross the highway, then follow it west for 125 feet before turning right and entering woods. **0.0**

S-N

N.Y. 52 (Stormville) to Taconic State Parkway

4.8 MILES

This section of the Trail is rocky, with many short ups and downs. It traverses the ridge of Stormville Mountain and the western side of Hosner Mountain. There are good views to the north over the Fishkill Plains, and west over the Hudson River Valley. During the Revolutionary War, the Fishkill area was an important supply center for the continental army, which was shielded from Redcoat troops by the Hudson Highlands.

The elevation at N.Y. 52 is 800 feet; at the Taconic State Parkway, 540 feet. The section's highest elevation is about 1,040 feet on Hosner Mountain.

Road Approaches—Both the northern and southern ends of this section are accessible by vehicle. Public transportation is not available at either end.

Maps—For route navigation, refer to Map 2 with this guide. For area detail, refer to the following USGS 7½-minute topographic quadrangles: Poughquag and Hopewell Junction, New York.

Shelters and Campsites—No shelters or campsites are available in this section, and no camping is permitted in the Trail corridor. Fires are not permitted.

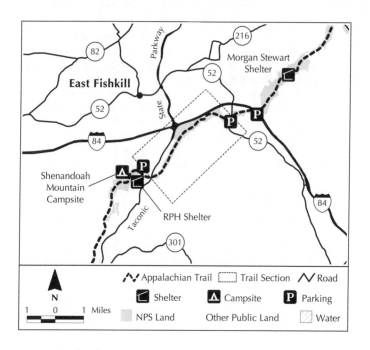

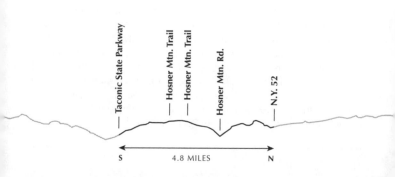

SECTION HIGHLIGHTS

Northern end of section →

At N.Y. 52, 0.4 mile west (compass-north) of the intersection of
N.Y. 52 with Leetown Road and 2.2 miles east (compass-south) of
Stormville (on Old N.Y. 52). Designated parking area located just
west of the Trail crossing. A store (open seven days a week) at the
northern end of the section, 0.5 mile east (compass-south) of the
Trail crossing, has groceries and sandwiches (follow N.Y. 52 south
for 0.4 mile, then turn right onto Leetown Road, and continue 0.1
mile to the store). Groceries and light meals also are available at a
store 2.0 miles east (compass-south) of the Trail crossing on N.Y. 52.
Stormville has a post office (ZIP Code 12582) and a meat market
that carries a limited supply of groceries, 2.2 miles west (compass-
north) of the crossing (proceed north on N.Y. 52 for 1.7 miles, then
turn right onto Old N.Y. 52, and continue for 0.5 mile). Another
store with a limited selection of groceries and a public telephone is
0.2 mile farther north, at the intersection of Old N.Y. 52 and N.Y.
216. No accommodations are available in this section. No public
transportation is available.

Hosner Mountain Road →

Leads west 0.2 mile to I-84 underpass and about two miles to Taconic
State Parkway. Leads east about two miles to N.Y. 52.

Fishkill Plains →

The fertile lands visible to compass-north of the Trail, known as the
Fishkill Plains, were purchased from native Americans in 1685 as
part of the "Rombout Patent." Under that deal, English and Dutch
settlers got 85,000 acres; the Indians got: "One hund Royalls, One
hund Pound Powder, Two hund fathom of White Wampum, thirty
tobacco boxes, ten holl adges, thirty Gunns, twenty Blankets, forty
fathom of Duffils, twenty fathom of stroudwater Cloth, thirty Kittles,
forty Hatchets, forty horns, forty shirts, forty p stockins, twelve coates
of R. B. & b. C., ten Drawing Knives, forty earthern Juggs, forty
Bottles, forty Knives, fouer ankers rum, ten halfe fatts Beere, two
hund tobacco Pipes, &c., Eighty Pound Tobaco."

N-S

TRAIL DESCRIPTION

0.0 At N.Y. 52, the **northern end of section**, southbound hikers leave the highway and begin a gradual ascent. Northbound hikers cross the highway (elev. 800 ft.), then follow it west for 125 feet before turning right and entering the woods (New York Section Four, above). **4.8**

0.3 Trail follows switchbacks over steep slope of Stormville Mountain. **4.5**

0.5 Northern summit of Stormville Mountain (elev. 1,056 ft.). **4.3**

0.8 Pass old trail to west. **4.0**

1.0 Reach viewpoint to right, over the Hudson River Valley, below the southern summit of Stormville Mountain. **3.8**

1.3 Trail follows switchbacks over steep section. **3.5**

1.6 Cross paved **Hosner Mountain Road** (elev. 400 ft.). Southbound hikers begin to ascend Hosner Mountain. Northbound hikers cross bridge over small brook and ascend Stormville Mountain. **3.2**

2.2 A.T. passes through large hemlock grove on west side of Hosner Mountain, below ridge. **2.6**

2.4 Cross rocky section, with views to north and west over the Hudson River Valley and the **Fishkill Plains**, with intersection of I-84 and the Taconic State Parkway visible below. **2.4**

S-N

SECTION HIGHLIGHTS

Hosner Mountain Side Trail →
Former A.T. route parallels relocated Trail but runs lower on the hillside. It rejoins the A.T. in 0.5 mile and may be used to make a circuit hike.

Hudson Highlands, Shawangunks, and Catskills →
The Catskills, northwest of the A.T. and west of the Hudson River near Kingston, New York, are one of New York's most scenic areas, and their streams and lakes provide drinking water for New York City. The Shawangunks, closer to the A.T., run along the west side of the Great Valley of the Appalachians, west of the Hudson near New Paltz. The American author Washington Irving, writing a tongue-in-cheek history of the exploration of New York in 1806, described the "awful defiles" of the Highlands that the early explorers of the Hudson River saw, "where it would seem that the gigantic Titans had erst waged their impious war with heaven, piling up cliffs on cliffs, and hurling vast masses of rock in wild confusion." Irving's description goes on to attempt a fanciful explanation of the geologic processes that produced the Highlands: "But in sooth, very different is the history of these cloud-capt mountains. These in ancient days before the Hudson poured his waters from the lakes, formed one vast prison, within whose rocky bosom the omnipotent Manetho [the native spirit Manitou] confined the rebellious spirits who repined at his control. Here bound in adamantine chains or jammed in rifted pines, or crushed by ponderous rocks, they groaned for many an age. At length the conquering Hudson, in his irresistible career towards the ocean, burst open their prison-house, rolling his tide triumphantly through its stupendous ruins.... When the elements are agitated by tempest, when the winds are up and the thunder rolls, then horrible is the yelling and howling of these troubled spirits, making the mountains to re-bellow with their hideous uproar; for at such times, it is said, they think the great Manetho is returning, once more to plunge them in gloomy caverns, and renew their intolerable captivity."

N-S

TRAIL DESCRIPTION

Hosner Mountain

2.9	Blue-blazed **Hosner Mountain Side Trail** intersects on the west side of the A.T.	1.9
3.1	Trail levels off (elev. 1,010 ft.) west of the summit of Hosner Mountain along a rocky ledge, with views to the west through the trees.	1.7
3.2	Pass a viewpoint (panorama of **Hudson Highlands, Shawangunks, and Catskills**) at top of rock steps.	1.6
3.4	Blue-blazed **Hosner Mountain Side Trail** intersects on the west side of the A.T.	1.4
3.5	Cross a small brook.	1.3
3.8	Pass a rocky viewpoint to the north and west above a steep section of Trail.	1.0

SECTION HIGHLIGHTS

Taconic State Parkway →

Originally promoted by Franklin D. Roosevelt (then a parks commissioner) as an extension of the Bronx River Parkway into the parkland of the Hudson Valley. Roosevelt contended against (and was defeated by) Robert Moses for funds to get it built in the 1920s. The parkway was completed in the early 1960s and today extends 105.3 miles, linking New York City with the counties of Westchester, Putnam, and Dutchess. Though the road was originally intended for pleasure driving, today it is an important commuter route to the city: About 25,000 vehicles per day follow the parkway past the A.T.

Southern end of section →

At the Miller Hill Road interchange of the Taconic State Parkway. Miller Hill Road leads west to the community of Shenandoah (no services). No parking is available at the parkway interchange. No accommodations or public transportation are available.

N-S

| TRAIL DESCRIPTION |

| 4.0 | Pass a stone wall to the east of the Trail, below a section of rock ledges and boulder outcroppings. | 0.8 |

| 4.6 | Pass through a hemlock grove. | 0.2 |

| 4.7 | A.T. intersects with paved Rockledge Road (elev. 540 ft.) below Hosner Mountain. Southbound hikers follow Rockledge Road parallel to the **Taconic State Parkway**. Northbound hikers enter woods to the right. | 0.1 |

| 4.8 | Reach paved Miller Hill Road with **Taconic State Parkway** underpass in view, the **southern end of section**. Southbound hikers turn right on Miller Hill Road and proceed across parkway (see New York Section Six below). Northbound hikers turn left on Rockledge Road. | 0.0 |

S-N

Taconic State Parkway to N.Y. 301

7.3 MILES

The Trail in this section passes over the summit of what is known locally as Shenandoah Mountain, a name derived from a native American word of arguable meaning. It has been translated as "Daughter of the Stars," "Silver Water," "River through the Spruces," "River of High Mountains," "Great Meadow," or "Big Flat Place." In any case, the mountain offers many good views on both sides of the Trail. The southern portion of the section passes through Clarence Fahnestock Memorial State Park, with a beautiful viewpoint over Canopus Lake. The elevation at the Taconic State Parkway is 540 feet; at N.Y. 301, it is 930 feet. The highest elevation on the section is 1,282 feet, at the summit of Shenandoah Mountain (also designated by the U.S. Geodetic Survey as "Looking Mountain").

Road Approaches—Both the northern and southern ends of this section are accessible by vehicle. The Trail is also accessible from Hortontown Road (mile 0.3 below, parking available) and Long Hill Road, which crosses the Trail at mile 2.7 below.

Maps—For route navigation, refer to Map 2 with this guide. For area detail, refer to the following USGS 7½-minute topographic quadrangles: Hopewell Junction and Oscawana Lake, New York. Another reference is NY–NJ TC East Hudson Trails Map 3.

Shelters and Campsites—This section of the Trail has one shelter, RPH Shelter, at mile 0.3 below. It also has one campsite, Shenandoah Tenting Area, at mile 1.6 below. A campground and campsites are located in Fahnestock State Park, at the southern end of the section, best reached from the A.T. on the side trail at mile 5.0 below.

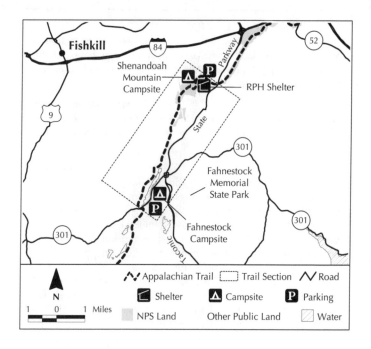

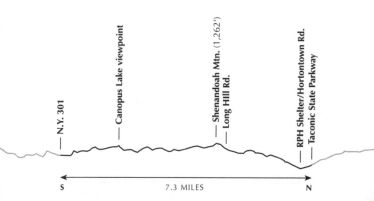

Northern end of section →

No parking is available at the parkway interchange, but parking is available at mile 0.3 below. Public transportation and public accommodations are not available.

Hortontown Road →

Leads west 0.2 mile to Miller Hill Road, near the community of Shenandoah (no services). Limited parking available near Trail crossing.

RPH Shelter →

A house acquired when the Trail corridor was purchased, and later adopted by the Ralph's Peak Hikers club in the early 1980's and converted into an overnight-use facility. It accommodates 10 in a three-sided cinder-block building with bunks; caretaker on duty in evenings from May to September; water (pump) and privy available. Shelter closes in winter, but tenting is permitted on grounds. Long-distance hikers may have postcards and letters sent to them at the shelter, c/o Joe Hrouda, 18 Memory Lane, Hopewell Junction, NY 12533. Packages are not accepted for delivery to hikers at the shelter. Next shelter: north, 9.0 miles (Morgan Stewart Memorial Shelter); south, 31.0 miles (West Mountain Shelter).

N-S

TRAIL DESCRIPTION

0.0　The **northern end of section** is at the Miller Hill Road underpass of the Taconic State Parkway. Southbound hikers proceed west on Miller Hill Road, then turn left steeply downhill just after crossing the southbound on-ramp of the parkway, and enter woods. Northbound hikers follow Miller Hill Road under the Taconic State Parkway and turn left on Rockledge Road, just past the northbound on-ramp of the parkway (New York Section Five above).　**7.3**

0.1　Cross bridge over a brook (elev. 480 ft.) just north of a hemlock grove where the Trail runs between stone walls.　**7.2**

0.3　Trail crosses **Hortontown Road**. Southbound hikers descend rock steps and continue 300 feet to where a side trail leads east to **RPH Shelter**.　**7.0**

0.5　Cross bridge over a brook on a hillside, near stone walls.　**6.8**

Footbridge in New York

S-N

SECTION HIGHLIGHTS

Shenandoah Mountain →

The mountain (also called Looking Mountain) shares a name with the community of Shenandoah, near the northern end of the section. According to a nineteenth-century history of Dutchess County, the first settler in Shenandoah kept a tavern and store there. One day, a traveling show stopped in the community, advertising a "recently imported animal from Africa, heretofore unknown to natural history, called a 'dodo.' This drew out a large crowd, but the dodo proved to be an imposture. The people thereupon tore down the tents, carried the dodo and a Shetland pony into the tavern, and told the showman he must refund the money or they would not deliver up his property. Finally a compromise was effected, by which the showman was allowed to proceed on his way… on condition of his treating the crowd." In recent years, areas at the northern foot of the mountain have been plagued by groundwater pollution from industrial solvents and are on the EPA Superfund list, but wells and streams on the mountain slope are free of that contamination. Still, purify your water.

Shenandoah Tenting Area →

On 0.1-mile side trail; water available from pump.

Long Hill Road →

No parking available. Leads west to East Fishkill (no services) and west to Hortontown Road.

Fahnestock State Park →

Named after Major Clarence Fahnestock, who bought the land from mining interests early in the 1900s. It was donated to the state of New York in 1929 by Dr. Ernest Fahnestock in memory of his brother, who was killed in World War I. Today, the park extends across more than 6,700 acres. The area was a patchwork of farms, iron mines, furnaces, and communities until the mid-nineteenth century.

N-S	TRAIL DESCRIPTION	
0.6	Cross a stream below a steep slope.	**6.7**
1.0	Pass through a hemlock grove.	**6.3**
1.2	Cross a stream.	**6.1**
1.3	Reach a high point on **Shenandoah Mountain**, with views through the trees to the east.	**6.0**
1.6	North of a stone wall and a steep slope, the Trail intersects in a clearing with a blue-blazed trail leading west to the **Shenandoah Tenting Area**.	**5.7**
1.9	Pass through a gap in a stone wall.	**5.4**
2.1	Cross a clearing for powerlines.	**5.2**
2.4	Cross an intermittent stream.	**4.9**
2.7	Cross **Long Hill Road**, near the boundary between Dutchess and Putnam counties.	**4.6**
3.0	Pass a viewpoint to the west.	**4.3**
3.1	Reach the open summit of **Shenandoah Mountain** (elev. 1,282 ft.), with beautiful views to the east and views through the trees to the west.	**4.2**
3.5	The Trail follows an old woods road, with a stone wall to the east.	**3.8**
4.2	Pass the ruins of a small stone building to the west of the Trail, just south of an intermittent stream.	**3.1**
4.3	The Trail intersects with a woods road in **Fahnestock State Park**. Southbound hikers bear right and leave the woods road. Northbound hikers continue straight ahead.	**3.0**

SECTION HIGHLIGHTS

Canopus Lake →

Impounded during the 1930s by the Civilian Conservation Corps in an area of old mines and named after a leader of the Wappinger Indians. A seasonal hot-dog and ice-cream stand is located at the beach at the northern end of the lake. Cold showers and swimming are also available. From the viewpoint overlooking Canopus Lake, proceed south on Trail for about 100 feet, then follow an unmarked trail steeply down to the lake shore, and proceed for about 0.2 mile along the shore. An access road on the eastern shore of the lake leads to N.Y. 301 and a campground across the highway, where tent sites are available.

Fahnestock Trail →

Leads west to Charcoal Burners Trail and into Hubbard-Perkins Conservation Area; the trailhead is on U.S. 9 (7.3 miles west), near McKeel Corners.

Southern end of section →

At N.Y. 301 in Fahnestock State Park. Campsites in the park are located on the southern side of N.Y. 301, 1.0 mile northeast of the Trail crossing. Hot showers, flush toilets, and rain shelters are available; no fee in tenting area for long-distance hikers. Ample parking is available 0.2 mile northeast of the Trail crossing on N.Y. 301. Public transportation is not available.

N-S

TRAIL DESCRIPTION

4.5 Cross a small stream. **2.8**

4.9 Side trails lead west to viewpoints. **2.4**

5.0 View to south over **Canopus Lake**, above a steep section **2.3**
of Trail. An unmarked trail leads east around the lake and
about 0.5 mile to a park campground.

5.3 Cross a small stream above the western shore of Canopus **2.0**
Lake, with views of the lake through the trees.

6.4 Cross a rocky stream along the ridge shoulder on the **0.9**
western side of Canopus Lake.

6.7 Blue-blazed **Fahnestock Trail** intersects on the west side **0.6**
of the A.T.

7.0 Pass a Trail register located on a tree to the east of the Trail **0.3**
(please sign), midway down a gradual slope.

7.2 A.T. intersects with N.Y. 301. Southbound hikers turn left **0.1**
and follow highway east. Northbound hikers turn right and
enter woods near a signboard east of the Trail.

7.3 Reach the **southern end of section** along N.Y. 301 at the **0.0**
southern end of Canopus Lake. Southbound hikers reenter
woods on south side of the highway (see New York Section Seven). Northbound hikers turn left and follow the
highway west.

S-N

N.Y. 301 to Canopus Hill Road

7.4 MILES

This section of the Trail passes through the highlands of Putnam County, New York, which was a center for iron mining along the Hudson until the mid-nineteenth century and played a crucial part in the Revolutionary War and Civil War. After its industry died out, the county actually lost population and became a vacation destination—fewer people lived there in 1920 than in 1820. Then, in the mid-twentieth century, its population grew again as it was rediscovered and settled by commuters to New York City.

Most of this section is in the Clarence Fahnestock Memorial State Park. At the northern end, the Trail follows a narrow-gauge railroad bed built in 1862 to transport ore from Sunk Mine to Cold Spring Turnpike. Elevation at N.Y. 301 is 930 feet; at Canopus Hill Road, 420 feet. The highest point is 1,061 feet, on the ridge between Sunk Mine Road and Dennytown Road.

Road Approaches—Both the northern and southern ends of this section are accessible by vehicle. Public transportation is not available at either end of this section.

Maps—For route navigation, refer to Map 2 with this guide. For area detail, refer to the following USGS 7½-minute topographic quadrangle: Oscawana Lake, New York. Another reference is NY-NJ TC East Hudson Trails Map 3.

Shelters and Campsites—This section of the Trail has two camping areas: Fahnestock State Park Campsites (northern end of section) and Dennytown Road Group Campsites (mile 3.7 below).

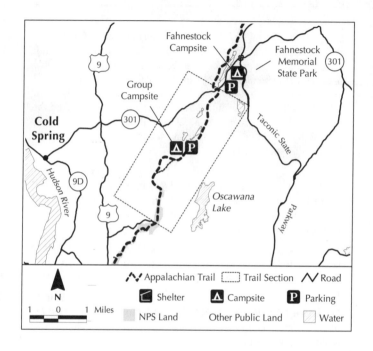

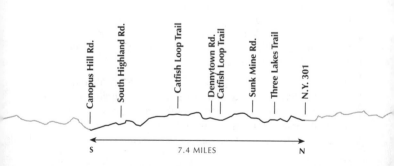

Northern end of section →

Parking is available along N.Y. 301, 0.2 mile northeast of the Trail crossing. No accommodations are available; food may be available seasonally at swimming area of Canopus Lake. Campsites maintained by Fahnestock State Park are available on the southern side of N.Y. 301, 1.0 mile northeast of the Trail crossing; hikers can avoid the road walk by using the side trail at page 80 above. Hot showers, flush toilets, and rain shelters are available; no fee in tenting area for long-distance hikers.

Mine railway →

Built in 1862 to bring ore from Sunk Mine to Dump Hill (located where Dennytown Road meets N.Y. 301), where it was dumped and shoveled into horse-drawn wagons for the final five-mile trip to the foundry at Cold Spring.

Old Mine Railroad Trail →

Leads 2.2 miles south to Sunk Mine Road, near Dennytown Road. This trail was temporarily closed in 2001 for ecological reasons.

Three Lakes Trail →

Leads east 1.3 miles back to N.Y. 301 at Canopus Lake and west 4.0 miles to Catfish Loop Trail, crossing the A.T. again near Dennytown Road (mile 3.7 below).

Sunk Mine →

Mining began in the area about 1755 along a vein of magnetic iron ore known as the Philipse vein. It was an important source of iron for the famous Cold Spring foundry near West Point, best known for producing the rifled cannon known as a "Parrott gun" during the Civil War. Sunk Mine got its name from the low-lying appearance of the land in one section.

Sunk Mine Road →

Sunk Mine Road leads west to the blue-blazed Three Lakes Trail, which can be used as an alternate hiking route back to N.Y. 301, and east about four miles past Clear Lake to Oscawana Lake.

N-S

TRAIL DESCRIPTION

0.0 **Northern end of section** at N.Y. 301, at southern tip of **7.4**
Canopus Lake. Southbound hikers descend rock steps and
turn right onto old **mine-railway** bed, passing a signboard
to west of Trail. Northbound hikers turn left and follow
N.Y. 301 west (New York Section Six above).

0.7 A.T. intersects with **mine-railway** bed just south of curved **6.7**
rock causeway. Southbound hikers turn left and leave
railway, soon beginning to ascend. Northbound hikers
turn right and follow the railway bed north. (Unblazed
Old Mine Railroad Trail continues compass-south along
the railway bed.)

0.9 A.T. crosses the blue-blazed **Three Lakes Trail** south of a **6.5**
mountain-laurel thicket.

1.1 Descend into ravine, then climb steeply out. **6.3**

1.3 Below the ridge, pass through an old field overgrown **6.1**
with barberry.

1.5 Trail leads along the crest of the ridge, with limited views **5.9**
on both sides of Trail, north of a hemlock grove.

1.9 Trail leads steeply over a low cliff. **5.5**

2.0 Cross a log bridge over a stream (outlet of a swamp to **5.4**
the west of the Trail) below a hemlock grove. On the
hillside beyond the swamp to the west are the old shafts
of **Sunk Mine**.

2.1 Reach **Sunk Mine Road** (many sections impassible for **5.3**
cars)**.** Southbound hikers turn right and follow the road
for 60 feet, then turn left onto a woods road and begin to
ascend. Northbound hikers turn right, follow the road for
60 feet, then turn left and enter a hemlock grove.

S-N

Catfish Loop Trail →

Leads south along an old woods road, crossing the A.T. again at mile 4.9 below, continuing south to Catfish Pond, and looping back to Dennytown Road (mile 3.7 below), for a total distance of 3.6 miles.

Dennytown Road →

Named after the Denny family, which operated an iron mine on the mountain to the east in the 1800s. The two stone buildings to the right were built during the 1920s or 1930s by an amateur stonemason. The larger building, which appears to resemble a chapel, reportedly was used as a chicken coop. Water is available from a spigot on the front wall of a smaller stone building adjacent to the road, 200 feet to east of the Trail. Parking is available near the road crossing. To reach this point by car, follow Dennytown Road south from N.Y. 301 for about 1.2 miles. To reach Dennytown Road Group Campsites, turn east on Dennytown Road for about 500 feet, then turn left on dirt road, and follow it to top of hill. The campsites are maintained for groups and thru-hikers by Fahnestock State Park. Water and latrines are available; no fee.

Three Lakes Trail →

Leads east 3.7 miles back to N.Y. 301 at Canopus Lake, crossing the A.T. at mile 0.9 above, and west 1.6 miles to Catfish Loop Trail, near the A.T.

Fahnestock State Park →

Named after Major Clarence Fahnestock, a physician who bought the land from mining interests early in the 1900s. After his death in World War I, his brother gave the land to the state. Today, the park extends over more than 6,700 acres. The area was a patchwork of farms, iron mines, furnaces, and communities until the mid-nineteenth century.

N-S

TRAIL DESCRIPTION

2.8 Reach high point of the ridge, with limited views to west.   **4.6**

3.2 Trail skirts a swamp (formerly a beaver pond).   **4.2**

3.4 Cross a stream (outlet of the swamp to west).   **4.0**

3.5 **Catfish Loop Trail**, blazed red, intersects on the east side of the A.T., across from a swampy area.   **3.9**

3.7 Cross **Dennytown Road**. Southbound hikers cross road and continue for 125 feet on joint route with blue-blazed **Three Lakes Trail**, then bear left (blue-blazed trail continues straight), and soon begin steady ascent. Northbound hikers descend from road through open field.   **3.7**

4.2 Pass a limited viewpoint to the east as the Trail tops a rise.   **3.2**

4.9 Cross the red-blazed **Catfish Loop Trail**.   **2.5**

5.2 Cross a stream. Southbound hikers follow an old woods road to the south. Northbound hikers parallel the stream, then ascend steeply.   **2.2**

5.3 A.T. intersects with old woods road. Southbound hikers turn right, leaving the old woods road, and descend. Northbound hikers turn left and ascend, following the old woods road, with a stream to the right.   **2.1**

5.6 A.T. intersects with old woods road. Southbound hikers turn right onto the woods road and descend. Northbound hikers turn left from the old road and ascend.   **1.8**

5.8 A.T. intersects with old woods road. Southbound hikers turn left, leaving the woods road. Northbound hikers turn right, following the woods road.   **1.6**

5.9 Cross a large boulder field, at the southern boundary of **Fahnestock State Park**.   **1.5**

S-N

South Highland Road →

Leads west about one mile to Old Albany Post Road and east 0.3 mile to Gilbert Corners (no services).

Stone foundations →

These served as a smallpox inoculation station for the Continental troops during the American Revolution.

Southern end of section →

Trail crossing is 0.3 mile west of intersection of Canopus Hill Road with Canopus Hollow Road. To reach the Trailhead, take U.S. 9 to Travis Corners Road. Proceed east on Travis Corners Road 0.8 mile to Old Albany Post Road. Turn right onto Old Albany Post Road, then left at the next intersection onto Canopus Hill Road. Continue east on Canopus Hill Road for one mile to the Trail crossing. Parking is not available here but is available at Dennytown Road, at mile 3.7 above. Light meals and a limited selection of groceries may be obtained from a store (open seven days a week) located at the intersection of Sunset Hill Road and Oscawana Lake Road, 1.6 miles east of the Trail crossing. To reach this store, go east on Canopus Hill Road for 0.3 mile to its intersection with Canopus Hollow Road, turn right (south) on Canopus Hollow Road for 0.1 mile, then turn left (east) on Sunset Hill Road, and follow it for 1.2 miles to its end at Oscawana Lake Road, where the store is located. *Note—Sunset Hill Road is a steep, narrow, winding road, with a climb of about 400 feet from Canopus Hollow Road.* No overnight accommodations are available in this section.

N-S

TRAIL DESCRIPTION

6.0 Reach a rocky knob, with limited views through the trees. **1.4**

6.4 Reach **South Highland Road**. Southbound hikers cross the road and ascend stone steps on the opposite side. Northbound hikers cross the road, descend to a stream, and cross a wooden bridge in 150 feet. **1.0**

7.4 **Southern end of section** is at paved Canopus Hill Road. On the north side of the road are Revolutionary-era **stone foundations** on either side of the Trail. To continue, southbound hikers cross the road and follow the Trail into the woods (see New York Section Eight below). Northbound hikers pass between old stone foundations and enter the woods. **0.0**

S-N

Canopus Hill Road to U.S. 9

5.0 MILES

The Trail climbs over Canopus Hill, Denning Hill, and Little Fort Hill and crosses the Old Albany Post Road. Elevation at Canopus Hill Road is 420 feet; at U.S. 9, it is 400 feet. The highest elevation is 900 feet at the top of Denning Hill.

This historic area saw considerable Revolutionary War activity. Canopus Valley Road and Old Albany Post Road were used by the Continentals to travel from Fishkill, a military supply depot, to Continental Village, three miles east of the Trail. The latter was the site of a troop encampment and still remains a small village. On October 9, 1777, the British moved north from Peekskill and routed 2,000 Continentals camped there. The men took to the surrounding hills, most of which were fortified. The names on the land—Fort Hill, Little Fort Hill, Fort Defiance Hill, Gallows Hill—are reminders of that time.

Road Approaches—Both the northern and southern ends of this section are accessible by vehicle. Parking is available at the southern end.

Maps—For route navigation, refer to Map 2 with this guide. For area detail, refer to the following USGS 7½-minute topographic quadrangles: West Point and Peekskill, New York. Additional references are NY-NJ TC East Hudson Trails Maps 1 and 3.

Shelters and Campsites—No designated shelters or campsites are located in this section, but camping for long-distance hikers is available on private property at the picnic pavilion of the old ball field of the Graymoor friary (mile 3.7 below). Campfires are not permitted.

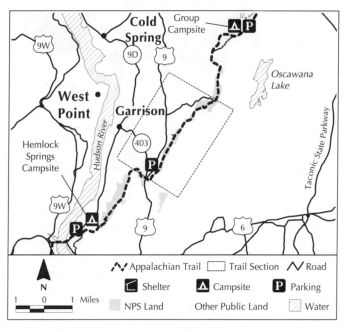

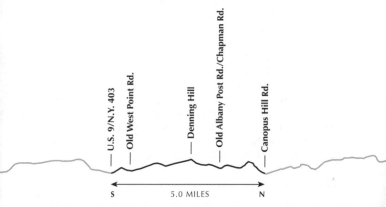

SECTION HIGHLIGHTS

Northern end of section →

The Trail crossing is 0.3 mile west of intersection of Canopus Hill Road with Canopus Hollow Road. To reach it, take U.S. 9 to Travis Corners Road. Proceed east on Travis Corners Road 0.8 mile to Old Albany Post Road. Turn right onto Old Albany Post Road, then left at the next intersection onto Canopus Hill Road. Continue east on Canopus Hill Road for one mile to the Trail crossing. Parking is not available here but is available at Dennytown Road, in New York Section Seven, above. Light meals and a limited selection of groceries may be obtained from a store (open seven days a week) located at the intersection of Sunset Hill Road and Oscawana Lake Road, 1.6 miles east of the Trail crossing. To reach this store, go east on Canopus Hill Road for 0.3 mile, turn right (south) on Canopus Hollow Road for 0.1 mile, then turn left (east) on Sunset Hill Road and follow it for 1.2 miles to its end at Oscawana Lake Road, where the store is located. Sunset Hill Road is a steep, narrow, winding road, with a climb of about 400 feet from Canopus Hollow Road.

Old Albany Post Road →

The 6.6-mile section of dirt road from Continental Village, New York, to U.S. 9, bisected by the A.T., has been recognized as one of the oldest unpaved roads in the nation still in use. A 1756 tavern, the Bird and Bottle, still operates today as an upscale restaurant and B&B, 2.8 miles west of the Trail crossing near Nelson Corners. The first path to Albany, following trails of Wappinger Indians, was scouted out by the Dutch in 1669. It was improved and became the Queen's Road during the reign of Queen Anne and, later, the King's Road during the reigns of Kings George I and II. In 1772, the provisional assembly instituted service by postal rider, and, during the Revolutionary War, George Washington regularly visited various outposts along the route. Stagecoach service began in 1785 and continued until 1851, when the Hudson River Railroad was completed to Albany. Newer sections of U.S. 9 have wiped out much of the historic route between Manhattan and Albany.

N-S	TRAIL DESCRIPTION	

0.0	The **northern end of section** is at paved Canopus Hill Road. Southbound hikers follow the footpath into the woods. Northbound hikers cross the road, pass between old stone foundations, and enter the woods (New York Section Seven above).	**5.0**
0.1	Cross a brook (elev. 350 ft.) below Canopus Hill.	**4.9**
0.4	Pass a large hemlock to the east of the Trail.	**4.6**
0.7	Reach a viewpoint in a cleared area at the top of Canopus Hill (elev. 820 ft.).	**4.3**
0.9	Cross several stone walls along a gradual slope.	**4.1**
1.4	Pass through a gap in a stone wall.	**3.6**
1.6	Pass through a blueberry patch above a steep section.	**3.4**
1.7	Reach dirt Chapman Road at its intersection with **Old Albany Post Road** (elev. 607 ft.). Southbound hikers cross the road, reenter the woods, cross a swampy area on puncheon, and ascend. Northbound hikers cross the road, then cross a wet area on rocks.	**3.3**
2.1	Trail leads steeply over rocks.	**2.9**
2.3	Steep, rocky area midway up Denning Hill.	**2.7**
2.5	Pass the summit of Denning Hill (elev. 960 ft.), with a good view to the east. On a clear day, you can see the New York City skyline—the northernmost point from which it is visible along the A.T. Southbound hikers continue along the ridge for 150 feet, then turn left and descend steeply. Northbound hikers descend and cross a stone wall.	**2.5**

SECTION HIGHLIGHTS

Hudson River →

First scouted in 1609 by Henry Hudson, searching for the fabled Northwest Passage, the Hudson soon became a vital passage into the interior of North America for settlers and helped make New York City a prime port. The view from Denning Hill shows the point at which the glacier-carved valley (the only fjord that the A.T. crosses) narrows, deepens, and cuts through the wall of the Hudson Highlands between Storm King Mountain, west of the river, and the village of Cold Spring, on the east bank. Consolidated Edison planned to build a power plant along the river, near Storm King, in the 1960s, but the plan was defeated by environmental activists.

Catskill Aqueduct →

South of Little Fort Hill, a Revolutionary War outpost, the Trail crosses the 92-mile-long aqueduct, which was tunneled through the hill in 1917. The aqueduct was built as a means of channeling water from the lakes and streams of the Catskills, under the Hudson River, and through the Highlands to New York City. It empties into Hillview Reservoir in Yonkers and Kensico Reservoir near White Plains, from which water goes to the city by way of tunnels drilled through the bedrock of Manhattan Island.

Graymoor →

The Friars of the Atonement and the Franciscan Sisters of the Atonement allow the picnic pavilion at the friary ball field to be used as a camping area by long-distance hikers. It is reached *via* an 0.4-mile blue-blazed trail that follows a paved road from the A.T. Water is available in the summer.

N-S

TRAIL DESCRIPTION

2.8 The A.T. follows a woods road. A blue-blazed side trail **2.2**
to the west leads 650 feet to an excellent view of the
Hudson River.

2.9 The A.T. intersects with a woods road. Southbound hik- **2.1**
ers reenter the woods on a footpath. Northbound hikers
follow the woods road.

3.0 The Trail leads steeply over rocks. Southbound hikers **2.0**
follow the ridge of Little Fort Hill, crossing the **Catskill
Aqueduct.** Northbound hikers follow a footpath through
the woods.

3.7 A short side trail marked with orange blazes leads east **1.3**
to a shrine on the property of the **Graymoor** friary, with
views to the east.

S-N

SECTION HIGHLIGHTS

Old West Point Road →

This road led to Benedict Arnold's headquarters at Garrison. Major John André, Arnold's liaison to the British army during the Revolutionary War, was taken down this road to be hanged after his and Arnold's plans to betray the Continental army were uncovered in 1780.

Southern end of section →

A restaurant is located 0.7 mile south on U.S. 9. Groceries and sandwiches are available at a store located at the intersection of U.S. 9 and South Mountain Pass, 1.9 miles south of the Trail crossing (open seven days a week). A variety of supplies and services is available in Peekskill, New York, about 4.8 miles from the southern end of the section (from the Trail crossing of U.S. 9, proceed south on U.S. 9 for 3.1 miles, then follow Highland Avenue to the center of Peekskill). Motels are available in Peekskill. Parking is available on a short road between U.S. 9 and N.Y. 403, about 0.1 mile north of the Trail crossing.

N-S

TRAIL DESCRIPTION

4.3   Trail reaches a private gravel road. Southbound hikers   0.7
       cross the road and follow it uphill. Northbound hikers
       cross the road, enter the woods, then pass through an
       overgrown field.

4.4   Cross unpaved **Old West Point Road**.   0.6

4.5   Pass a paved road with blue blazes near an open field,   0.5
       leading compass-south to the Graymoor friary and its ball-
       field camping area. Southbound hikers continue across
       another grassy area with a red shed on one side and re-
       enter the woods, descending steeply. Northbound hikers
       continue across a grassy area and enter the woods.

4.8   Cross paved Old Highland Turnpike, to the north of a   0.2
       swampy area that the Trail crosses on puncheon.

5.0   Reach the **southern end of section** at the intersection of   0.0
       U.S. 9 and N.Y. 403. Southbound hikers continue across
       road and cement traffic island, cross N.Y. 403, and follow
       puncheon across pasture (see New York Section Nine,
       below). Northbound hikers enter woods on footpath.

S-N

U.S. 9 to Bear Mountain Bridge

5.8 MILES

The Trail leads along trails and old carriage roads through woodland in the northern part of the section, with a fine viewpoint over the Hudson River. Do not be surprised to see evidence of horses in this area, as they are permitted on the carriage roads (but not on the trails) of Hudson Highlands State Park. At the southern end of the section, the route traverses the steep western slope of the ridge known as Anthony's Nose and crosses Bear Mountain Bridge. Elevation at U.S. 9 is 400 feet; at Bear Mountain Bridge, elevation is 176 feet. The highest elevation is 840 feet, on Canada Hill.

Road Approaches—Both the northern and southern ends are accessible by road. Note that this area has three "Route 9s"—U.S. 9 (the "New York–Albany Post Road") crosses the Trail at the northern end. N.Y. 9D, which the Trail follows at the southern end, runs parallel to and near the Hudson River on the eastern side of the river and ends at the Bear Mountain Bridge. U.S. 9W is on the western side of the river.

Maps—For route navigation, refer to Maps 2 and 3 with this guide. For area detail, refer to the following USGS 7½-minute topographic quadrangle: Peekskill, New York. Another reference is NY-NJ TC East Hudson Trails Map 1.

Shelters and Campsites—This section has one campsite, Hemlock Springs Campsite, at mile 3.6 below, and camping is not permitted elsewhere in the section. There are no shelters. Campfires are permitted only at designated campsite fireplaces.

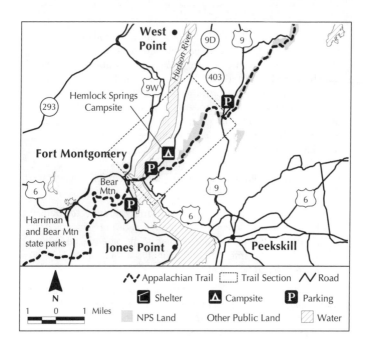

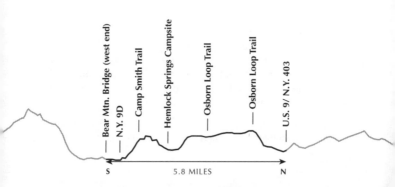

Northern end of section →

The Trail crosses U.S. 9 near Peekskill, 4.0 miles north of the intersection of U.S. 9 with U.S. 6/202. Parking is available on a short road between U.S. 9 and N.Y. 403, about 0.1 mile north of the Trail crossing. No public transportation is available. A restaurant is located 0.7 mile south on U.S. 9. Groceries and sandwiches are available at a store located at the intersection of U.S. 9 and South Mountain Pass, 1.9 miles south of the Trail crossing (open seven days a week). Motel accommodations and a variety of supplies and services are available in Peekskill, south of the Trail crossing of U.S. 9. (From the crossing, walk south on U.S. 9 for 3.1 miles, then follow Highland Avenue to the center of Peekskill.)

Carriage Connector Trail →

Leads 0.9 mile west (compass-north) into Hudson Highlands State Park, bypassing White Rock and leading to the blue-blazed Osborn Loop Trail, and 1.1 mile farther downhill to a trailhead at N.Y. 9D *via* the red-blazed Sugarloaf Trail.

Hudson Highlands State Park →

Mostly undeveloped, the park offers fishing, boating, and 25 miles of hiking trails. Numerous old carriage roads (open to horses) are found in the park; some are even used for the A.T.

Osborn Loop Trail →

Runs west (compass-north) of the A.T. 3.8 miles, rejoining the A.T. at mile 2.4 below. It can be combined with the A.T. to make a loop hike. The Osborn Preserve is a part of Hudson Highlands State Park just west of the A.T. The site of the ruined Beverly Robinson house is at the north foot of Sugarloaf Hill. The Tory officer's estate was commandeered by Washington, Lafayette, Hamilton, and Arnold during the Revolution and was Arnold's home at the time his plot to betray the Continental Army was uncovered.

Curry Pond Trail →

A short connecting trail between the A.T. and the Osborn Loop.

N-S	TRAIL DESCRIPTION	
0.0	The **northern end of section** is at the intersection of U.S. 9 with N.Y. 403. Southbound hikers follow puncheon across pasture until the Trail intersects with an old carriage road. Northbound hikers cross a cement traffic island and U.S. 9 and enter woods on footpath (see New York Section Eight above).	**5.8**
0.5	The A.T. intersects on the west side of the Trail with the yellow-blazed **Carriage Connector Trail** leading to **Hudson Highlands State Park**. Southbound hikers turn left, leaving the carriage road, and ascend, steeply in places, on a footpath. Northbound hikers turn right as the A.T. follows an old carriage road.	**5.3**
1.0	Blue-blazed **Osborn Loop Trail** intersects on the west side of the A.T. Southbound hikers bear left onto a carriage road over White Rock. Northbound hikers bear right, leaving the carriage road, and descend, steeply in places, on a footpath.	**4.8**
1.1	Blue-blazed side trail leads west 100 feet to a beautiful viewpoint over the Hudson River, with the Bear Mountain Bridge visible to the south and West Point visible to the north.	**4.7**
1.9	Yellow-blazed **Curry Pond Trail** intersects on the west side of the A.T., leading to the Osborn Loop Trail and **Manitoga,** a private nature preserve.	**3.9**
2.3	Unmarked side trail departs from the east side of the A.T. at a curve in the Trail.	**3.5**
2.4	The blue-blazed **Osborn Loop Trail** intersects on the west side of the A.T. Southbound hikers turn left, leaving the old carriage road, and continue on a footpath. Northbound hikers bear right onto a carriage road.	**3.4**

SECTION HIGHLIGHTS

Manitoga →
A privately owned preserve with hiking trails open to the public that lead through a woodland area landscaped by the noted decorative designer Russel Wright.

South Mountain Pass Road →
Groceries and sandwiches are available at a store located at the intersection of U.S. 9 and South Mountain Pass, which may be reached by following South Mountain Pass east for 1.7 miles. Parking for five cars is available here.

Hemlock Springs Campsite →
100 feet east of A.T., with nearby spring. This ridgetop campsite offers some views of the Hudson. Most of the hemlocks in this area are dead or dying from an infestation of woolly adelgids. Nice tentsites are tucked away in the woods; do not camp in the open area where the blue-blazed trail leaves the A.T.

Camp Smith Trail →
Leads east 0.5 mile to the summit of Anthony's Nose and continues 3.2 miles to U.S. 6. Activities at the camp may result in trail closures.

Anthony's Nose →
Many accounts speculate on the naming of Anthony's Nose, a prominent ridge with impressive views overlooking the Hudson where the river cuts through the Highlands at Bear Mountain. Early historians believed it was named in 1525 by a Portuguese sailor, who referred to the river as "Rio St. Antonio." The village of Manitou, north of the bridge, was once called St. Anthonysville. Washington Irving's version in Diedrich Knickerbocker's *History of New York* claims it was named for Anthony Van Corlear, or Anthony the Trumpeter. Some believe that it was named for General "Mad" Anthony Wayne, who led the successful march to capture Stony Point from the British in 1779. (A trail in the Harriman and Bear Mountain state parks follows the march's route.)

N-S	TRAIL DESCRIPTION	
2.5	Trail crosses a high point near the summit of Canada Hill.	**3.3**
3.0	Negotiate a steep section between Canada Hill and South Mountain Pass.	**2.8**
3.3	Pass a Trail register (please sign).	**2.5**
3.4	A.T. intersects with **South Mountain Pass Road** (a dirt road). The Trail follows the road for 250 feet. Southbound hikers leave South Mountain Pass Road on a dirt road and pass a massive steel gate that blocks the road. Northbound hikers reenter the woods and ascend.	**2.4**
3.6	A.T. intersects with a dirt road in a "Y" intersection. Southbound hikers take the right fork and shortly reach an open area. A blue-blazed side trail leads to **Hemlock Springs Campsite**.	**2.2**
3.7	After a descent, cross a brook, and ascend.	**2.1**
3.9	Trail follows switchbacks on a steep section near the stone embankment of a road.	**1.9**
4.4	Trail intersects with a rocky dirt road at a curve in the road. Southbound hikers continue ahead on the dirt road. Northbound hikers leave the dirt road, continuing ahead on the footpath. Be careful not to miss this turn: The road leads into Camp Smith, and trespassers will be arrested.	**1.4**
4.6	The blue-blazed **Camp Smith Trail**, which leads to the summit of **Anthony's Nose**, intersects on the east side of the A.T. Southbound hikers turn right, leaving the dirt road they have been following, and begin a steep descent on a footpath. Northbound hikers follow A.T. left onto the dirt road after the ascent.	**1.2**

Bear Mountain Bridge →

After Bear Mountain State Park opened in 1916, traffic crossing the Hudson here overwhelmed existing ferry services, and the bridge was proposed as a solution. It was authorized in 1922 and opened to traffic in 1924, though it never proved a money-maker as hoped. At the time of its completion in 1924, Bear Mountain Bridge's 2,332-foot length made it the longest suspension bridge in the world. Its towers rise 351 feet, its roadway lies 135 feet above the river, and more than 7,000 miles of cable were employed in its construction. It has been designated a national engineering landmark as an important precursor to the twentieth century's great suspension bridges.

Southern end of section →

At the tollgate at the southern (compass-west) end of the Bear Mountain Bridge. No parking is available here, but parking is available along the shoulder of N.Y. 9D about 0.2 mile south) of the point where the Trail leaves N.Y. 9D and ascends Anthony's Nose. Parking is also available at the Bear Mountain Inn, 0.8 mile south of the tollgate (fee charged in summer). Bus service to New York City *via* Short Line Bus System, (201) 444-7005, is also available there. Limited rail service (weekends only) to New York City (Grand Central Terminal) *via* the Metro-North Railroad, (212) 532-4900 or (800) 638-7646, is available at Manitou, 1.6 miles north of the point where the Trail leaves N.Y. 9D and begins its ascent of Anthony's Nose. Accommodations and meals are available at the Bear Mountain Inn, and a post office (ZIP Code 10911) is near the inn. Fort Montgomery, New York, has meals, groceries, and a post office (ZIP Code 10922) 0.7 mile compass-north of the Bear Mountain Bridge tollgate on U.S. 9W. Supplies, services, and accommodations are also available in Peekskill, 4.0 miles east (compass-south) of the bridge's north end (mile 5.3 above) *via* U.S. 6/202.

N-S

TRAIL DESCRIPTION

View from Bear Mountain Bridge

5.1 A.T. intersects with paved N.Y. 9D. Southbound hikers turn left and follow the highway, walking facing traffic to where the road widens to accommodate parking. Cross here (it is unsafe to cross close to the bridge). Northbound hikers cross the highway at the Westchester–Putnam county line, and begin a steady ascent that is steep in places.   **0.7**

5.3 North (compass-east) end of **Bear Mountain Bridge**. Southbound hikers cross the bridge on the north walkway. Northbound hikers turn left on N.Y. 9D and continue along the road, facing traffic.   **0.5**

5.8 The **southern end of section** is at the south (compass-west) end of **Bear Mountain Bridge**. Southbound hikers turn at the crosswalk just beyond the toll booth and follow the walkway through Trailside Museums and Zoo (New York Section Ten below). Northbound hikers proceed compass-east, crossing the bridge.   **0.0**

S-N

Bear Mountain Bridge to Arden Valley Road (Tiorati Circle)

13.1 MILES

The Trail passes through the northern portion of Harriman and Bear Mountain state parks, including the Trailside Museums, where it descends to 124 feet above sea level, the lowest elevation on the entire A.T. It then climbs to the summit of Bear Mountain (elev. 1,305 ft.) and later crosses West, Black, Letterrock, and Goshen mountains. Many beautiful views of the Hudson Valley and the Highlands can be seen from the summits and ridges of those mountains.

Harriman Trails: A Guide and History, published by the New York–New Jersey Trail Conference, offers more detail on side trails.

Road Approaches—Both the northern and southern ends of this section are accessible by vehicle.

Maps—For route navigation, refer to Map 3 with this guide. For area detail, refer to the following USGS 7½-minute topographic quadrangles: Peekskill and Popolopen Lake, New York. Another reference is NY-NJ TC Trail Map 4 (Harriman Park–North Half).

Shelters and Campsites—This section has two shelters: West Mountain Shelter, at mile 5.8 below, and William Brien Memorial Shelter, at mile 8.9 below. Camping is not permitted elsewhere in the section. Campfires are permitted only at fireplaces in designated shelters.

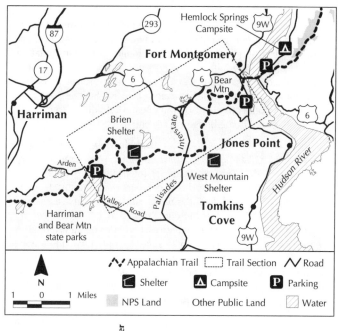

Appalachian Trail   Trail Section   Road
Shelter   Campsite   Parking
N   1   0   1   Miles
NPS Land   Other Public Land   Water

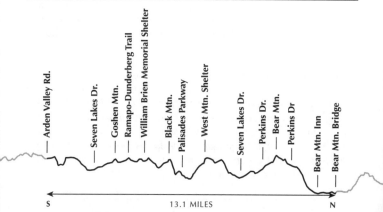

S   13.1 MILES   N

Northern end of section →
Ample parking (fee charged) in summer is available at the Bear
Mountain Inn, at mile 0.8 below. Food, lodging, and transportation
are available at the inn. Meals, groceries, accommodations, and
a post office (ZIP Code 10922) are available in the village of Fort
Montgomery, 0.7 mile to the north along U.S. 9W. Supplies, services,
and accommodations are also available in Peekskill, 4.0 miles east
(compass-south) of the bridge's north end (page 105 above).

Trailside Museums and Zoo →
Opened in 1927 as a collaboration between the American Museum
of Natural History and the Palisades Interstate Park Commission,
realizing Benton MacKaye's dream of nature trails and study centers
along the A.T. Today it includes nature and geology museums and
the Fort Clinton Historical Museum, as well as a children's zoo, in
which many of the animals were rescued after being crippled. A
fee is charged; long-distance hikers are exempted when following
the A.T. through. Fort Clinton and nearby Fort Montgomery were
important outposts during the Revolution. At Fort Montgomery, the
Continentals strung a chain across the Hudson in 1777 in a failed
attempt to stymie advancing British naval forces.

Walt Whitman
The statue's verses from "Song of the Open Road," are perhaps a nod to
A.T. pioneer Raymond F. Torrey, whose influential New York outdoors
column, "The Long Brown Path," took its title from the poem.

Note—*When Trailside's gates are closed, the A.T. route skirts the
fenced complex to compass-north and west. Southbound hikers
continue straight from the bridge to the traffic circle, bear left, cross
U.S. 9W, and proceed to Hessian Lake, then follow a paved path
along the lake's eastern shore until the A.T. is reached toward the
lake's southern end. Northbound hikers follow the paved path along
the east shore of Hessian Lake to the traffic circle and cross 9W there
to reach tollgate of Bear Mountain Bridge.*

N-S

TRAIL DESCRIPTION

Walt Whitman statue at Trailside

0.0 The **northern end of section** is at the toll plaza on the west end of the Bear Mountain Bridge. Southbound hikers turn left, pass through north gate of **Trailside Museums and Zoo**, and follow white blazes along paved paths past the statue of **Walt Whitman** to a gate on the south side of the zoo, and an underpass (mile 0.3 below). Northbound hikers proceed across the Bear Mountain Bridge (see New York Section Nine above). When gates are closed, the official A.T. route skirts the Trailside complex (see note on opposite page). **13.1**

0.3 The Trail passes under U.S. 9W *via* a tunnel. Southbound hikers follow paved trails toward **Bear Mountain Inn** (mile 0.8 below). Northbound hikers turn right after tunnel, then left, passing a refreshment stand, then enter the gates of **Trailside Museums and Zoo**, following white blazes along paved path past statue of **Walt Whitman** to gate on north side of zoo (mile 0.0 above). When the gates are closed, the official A.T. route skirts the Trailside complex (see note on opposite page). **12.8**

S-N

Bear Mountain Inn →

Built in 1915 as part of the Palisades Interstate Park, the inn offers food and accommodations (reservations required). Parking for hikers is available (fee charged in summer). Bus service to New York City is available *via* Short Line Bus System, (201) 444-7005. The post office for Bear Mountain (ZIP Code 10911) and the headquarters of Harriman and Bear Mountain state parks are near the Inn. The Major Welch Trail (see mile 3.2 below) provides an alternate route up Bear Mountain.

Ski jump →

Now defunct, the jump hosted more ski-jump competitions than any other "hill" in the United States before it was closed in the 1970s.

Suffern–Bear Mountain Trail →

Leads compass-southwest 23.5 miles between Bear Mountain Inn and Suffern.

Bear Mountain →

Relocations of the A.T. route up Bear Mountain are planned for 2003 and 2004. The blazed route may differ from this guide. Perkins Memorial Tower, at the summit, was built in 1934 in memory of George W. Perkins, first president of the Palisades Interstate Park Commission, and offers views of the New York City skyline (compass-south), the Ramapo Hills (compass-west), and the Hudson Highlands (compass-east). A plaque near the summit commemorates Joseph Bartha, a pioneering trail builder.

Major Welch Trail →

Leads 2.6 miles from Perkins Drive across the summit of Bear Mountain to Bear Mountain Inn (see mile 0.8 above). Major William Welch, general manager and chief engineer of Harriman and Bear Mountain state parks from 1910 to 1940, also served as the first chairman of the Appalachian Trail Conference. He designed the metal marker and "A-over-T" monogram that became the standard symbol of the Appalachian Trail, now an ATC trademark.

N-S	TRAIL DESCRIPTION	
0.8	The Trail crosses a playground area at the southern end of Hessian Lake, near the **Bear Mountain Inn** at the foot of Bear Mountain. The A.T. intersects there with the **Major Welch Trail**, Cornell Trail, and **Suffern-Bear Mountain (S-BM) Trail**. Southbound hikers follow the paved path (jointly with the yellow-blazed S-BM Trail) uphill. Northbound hikers follow the paved path along the shore of Hessian Lake.	**12.3**
1.0	Cross under a former **ski jump**.	**12.1**
1.4	The yellow-blazed **Suffern–Bear Mountain Trail** intersects to the east partway up Bear Mountain. Southbound hikers turn right and ascend, leaving the S-BM Trail; northbound hikers descend, following the A.T. and S-BM.	**11.7**
1.8	Reach an abandoned paved road above a steep slope, with views of Hudson River, Bear Mountain Bridge, Bear Mountain Inn, and Iona Island.	**11.3**
2.1	The Trail follows a flight of rock steps.	**11.0**
2.3	Cross Scenic Drive twice.	**10.8**
2.6	Summit of **Bear Mountain** (elev. 1,305 ft.). Southbound hikers continue along the edge of a paved road. Northbound hikers turn right, passing a plaque, and begin their descent.	**10.5**
3.2	The A.T intersects with paved Perkins Drive near the **Major Welch Trail**. Southbound hikers follow the road downhill. Northbound hikers leave road and follow A.T. toward summit of Bear Mountain.	**9.9**

SECTION HIGHLIGHTS

Fire Closures—*During very dry periods, some trails in the Harriman and Bear Mountain state parks may be closed to the public to prevent forest fires; however, the A.T. should remain open under agreements with the Trail community. Hikers are advised to consult staff members at park headquarters at Bear Mountain or at the stone building at the Tiorati Circle for current information.*

1777 Trail →

Leads 10.7 miles between the Trailside Museums, the Popoplen viaduct of U.S. 9W, and Jones Point, following the route of the British assault in 1777 on Forts Clinton and Montgomery.

Fawn Trail →

Leads west 0.7 mile to Anthony Wayne Recreation Area, with parking, picnic areas with fireplaces, and playing fields.

Harriman State Park →

The portion of the A.T. crossing Harriman State Park was the first section of the Trail to be completed. It officially opened on Sunday, October 7, 1923. Financier and railroad magnate Edward R. Harriman (1848-1909), who owned immense tracts of land here and in Sterling Forest farther south, conceived the idea of establishing a park in this area. In 1908, the state of New York acquired land around Bear Mountain to erect a prison. Due to the historical significance and scenic beauty of this land, the public objected to this proposal. Finally, in 1910, Harriman's widow, Mary A. Harriman, agreed to donate 10,000 acres of land to the state on the condition the state abandon its plan to establish a prison at Bear Mountain (Sing Sing prison was later built at Ossining). Harriman and Bear Mountain state parks expanded considerably in succeeding years, and many improvements were made under the supervision of Major William Welch. Today, the two parks encompass 52,000 acres.

N-S

TRAIL DESCRIPTION

3.7 The A.T. intersects with paved Perkins Drive. Southbound hikers leave the road and enter the woods. Northbound hikers follow the road uphill. **9.4**

4.2 Cross Seven Lakes Drive. Southbound hikers briefly follow a wide woods road, the route of the red-on-white blazed **1777 Trail**. Northbound hikers begin ascent of Bear Mountain. **8.9**

4.3 The A.T. follows a woods road, now a cross-country ski trail. **8.8**

4.5 The red-blazed **Fawn Trail** intersects to the west, at the foot of West Mountain in **Harriman State Park**. Southbound hikers begin steep ascent. **8.6**

5.0 Viewpoint on West Mountain looks compass-east and southeast over Bear Mountain and Hudson River. **8.1**

Harriman State Park

S-N

Timp–Torne Trail →

Extends 10.9 miles between the scenic cliff south of here known as the Timp and Popolopen Torne, a summit north of Bear Mountain with a panoramic view. For 0.7 mile, the T-T route follows the A.T. "Torne" is a locally common word, apparently of Dutch origin, used to describe a rocky summit.

West Mountain Shelter →

Stone structure built in 1928; accommodates 8; water may be available from an unreliable spring 0.4 mile farther on the Timp-Torne Trail (steep descent required—not recommended). Next shelter: north, 31.0 miles (RPH Shelter); south, 3.1 miles (William Brien Memorial Shelter).

Ramapo-Dunderberg Trail →

Extends 21.4 miles, from Tuxedo to U.S. 9W, just south of Jones Point, *via* Tiorati Circle, and runs concurrently with A.T. for 4.2 miles. It is the oldest hiking trail in the park.

Palisades Interstate Parkway →

A scenic four-lane parkway extending 42 miles from the George Washington Bridge to Bear Mountain. Cross with care—traffic here is more than 30,000 vehicles per day.

1779 Trail →

Blazed blue-on-white. The trail follows the route Gen. "Mad Anthony" Wayne's Continental army took in 1779 to attack Stony Point and leads 8.6 miles between the Poplopen viaduct and Bulsontown.

N-S

	TRAIL DESCRIPTION	

5.1 The blue-blazed **Timp-Torne (T-T) Trail** intersects to the   **8.0**
west, near the high point on West Mountain (elev. 1,146
ft.) and viewpoint over Bear Mountain and Hudson River.
Northbound hikers begin steep descent.

5.4 The Trail crosses a long, flat rock on West Mountain, near   **7.7**
rock ledges with good views to the west.

5.8 The blue-blazed **Timp-Torne (T-T) Trail** intersects to the   **7.3**
east at a high point atop West Mountain. **West Mountain
Shelter** is 0.6 mile to the east *via* the T-T Trail.

6.3 Cross Beechy Bottom Road, marked with blue-on-white   **6.8**
plastic blazes as a bike path.

6.5 Cross a stream, a water source, 200 feet north of a woods   **6.6**
road marked with blue-on-white plastic blazes as a bike
path and with red-plastic blazes as a cross-country ski
trail.

6.6 Cross Beechy Bottom Brook on a wooden bridge.   **6.5**

6.7 The red-on-white-blazed **Ramapo-Dunderberg (R-D)**   **6.4**
Trail intersects on the east side of the A.T. (Southbound
hikers follow the two trails, which run concurrently to
mile 9.7 below.)

6.8 Cross **Palisades Interstate Parkway**.   **6.3**

7.1 Cross the **1779 Trail** compass-east of the steep slope of   **6.0**
Black Mountain.

7.5 Cross open rocks on the south side of Black Mountain,   **5.6**
with beautiful views of Hudson River to the east and New
York City to the south.

7.9 Reach an overlook, just compass-east of a steep section,   **5.2**
with views to compass-northwest over Silvermine Lake.

S-N

William Brien Memorial Shelter →

Water from spring-fed well on blue-blazed trail 250 feet from shelter (may fail in dry weather; water available at Tiorati Circle). Named in memory of the first president of the New York Ramblers, William Brien. An original shelter at Island Pond was removed and the name transferred to this shelter, beneath the rocky slope of Leterrock Mountain, a glacially formed *roche moutonée*. Next shelter: north, 3.1 miles (West Mountain Shelter); south, 5.3 miles (Fingerboard Shelter).

Menomine Trail →

Leads west (compass-north) 2.4 miles, past picnic and restroom facilities at Silvermine Lake, to connect with the Long Path, and east (compass-south) 0.9 mile to connect with the Red Cross Trail.

Lake Tiorati →

Tiorati means "sky-like" in the Algonkian language. This lake formerly consisted of two bodies of water, Cedar Pond and Little Cedar Pond. They were first dammed in 1767 by Peter Hasenclever to provide a power source for his mines and then, 150 years later, combined to form Lake Tiorati.

Seven Lakes Drive →

Leads east (compass-southwest) to Lake Tiorati and Tiorati Circle and west (compass-northeast) to Palisades Interstate Parkway and Anthony Wayne Recreation Area.

Southern end of section →

The Trail crosses Arden Valley Road 0.3 mile west of its intersection with Seven Lakes Drive at the Tiorati Circle. No parking is available at the Trail crossing, but ample parking is available at Tiorati Circle (fee charged in summer). No public transportation is available. Refreshments may be obtained during the summer at Tiorati Circle, where a ranger station, bathing beach, and a public phone are located as well. Water is available from early May until November 1 from a faucet at the northeast corner of the circle.

N-S	TRAIL DESCRIPTION	

8.0	Cross a fire road, now a cross-country ski trail, in the saddle between Letterrock and Black mountains.	**5.1**
8.8	Cross rocky high point on Letterrock Mountain (elev. 1,140 ft.).	**4.3**
8.9	Pass **William Brien Memorial Shelter** at foot of rocky slope, near intersection of yellow-blazed **Menomine Trail**.	**4.2**
9.2	Reach rocky clearing atop hill, with views through trees to left.	**3.9**
9.7	Cross rocks over wet area in saddle between Goshen and Letterrock mountains. Red-on-white-blazed **Ramapo-Dunderberg (R-D) Trail** intersects on east side of A.T. and leads compass-southwest to **Lake Tiorati**. (Northbound hikers follow the two trails, which run concurrently to mile 6.7 above.)	**3.4**
10.8	A.T. route follows fire road.	**2.3**
10.9	Cross **Seven Lakes Drive**, and reenter the woods.	**2.2**
11.1	Cross bridge over stream below Stockbridge Mountain.	**2.0**
11.3	Trail turns sharply and switches back.	**1.8**
11.9	Reach a rocky promontory on a shoulder of Stockbridge Mountain; the view to the compass-south is over Lake Tiorati.	**1.2**
12.7	Cross rocks below the ridge of Fingerboard Mountain, which the A.T. skirts.	**0.4**
13.1	The **southern end of section** is at Arden Valley Road. Southbound hikers continue across the paved road and reenter woods (see New York Section Eleven, below). Northbound hikers ascend into the woods.	**0.0**

Arden Valley Road (Tiorati Circle) to N.Y. 17 (Arden)

5.5 MILES

The Trail here passes through Harriman State Park and an area abounding in disused shafts, pits, and dumps of old iron mines, some of which date back to 1730. The history of mining in the highlands is long and interesting, and some of it is noted below.

The route of the Trail in this section has an interesting history as well. The original route—first constructed in 1922–23—remained essentially the same for many years and is the earliest part of the A.T. to be completed. However, in the late 1970s, Island Pond became littered and unsightly. The ensuing relocation around the southern end of the lake eliminated all views of the lake and was considered boring by most hikers. In 1993, the local A.T. management committee decided to reroute the Trail a short distance inland from the original route around the northern end of the lake.

The elevation of the Trail at Arden Valley Road at the northern end of the section is 1,196 feet, and, at N.Y. 17, it is 565 feet. The highest point on this section is 1,328 feet, at the summit of Fingerboard Mountain.

Maps—For route navigation, refer to Map 3 with this guide. For area detail, refer to the following USGS 7½-minute topographic quadrangles: Popolopen Lake and Monroe, New York. Another reference is NY–NJ TC Trail Map 4 (Harriman Park—North Half).

Shelters and Campsites—This section has one shelter: Fingerboard Shelter, mile 1.1 below. Camping is not permitted elsewhere in the section. Campfires are permitted only at established fireplaces.

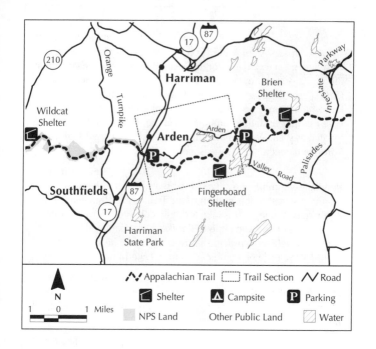

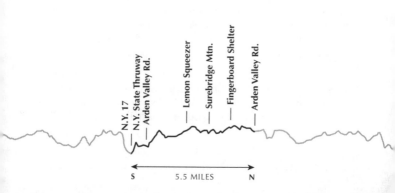

SECTION HIGHLIGHTS

Northern end of section →

The A.T. crosses Arden Valley Road 0.3 mile west of its intersection with Seven Lakes Drive (Tiorati Circle). No parking is available at the Trail crossing; however, ample parking is available at the Tiorati Circle (fee charged in season). No public transportation is available. Refreshments may be obtained during the summer at Tiorati Circle, where a ranger station, bathing beach, and public telephone are located as well. Water is available from early May until November 1 from a faucet at the northeast corner of the circle.

Tiorati Circle →

Popular swimming and picnicking area near a traffic circle. Lake Tiorati, just east of this section of the Trail, means "sky-like" in the Algonkian language. This lake formerly consisted of two bodies of water, Cedar Pond and Little Cedar Pond, first dammed in 1767 by Peter Hasenclever to provide a power source for his iron mines and then, 150 years later, combined to form Lake Tiorati.

Ramapo–Dunderberg Trail →

Extends 21.4 miles from Tuxedo to U.S. 9W, just south of Jones Point, and runs concurrently with A.T. for 4.2 miles. It is the oldest hiking trail in the park.

Fingerboard Shelter →

Stone structure built in 1928; accommodates 8; water from Lake Tiorati (0.5 mile to the east) or from a water faucet (summer only) at the Tiorati Circle (0.3 mile east of A.T. crossing of Arden Valley Road; 1.4 miles north of shelter). Next shelter: north, 5.3 miles (William Brien Memorial Shelter); south, 14.3 miles (Wildcat Shelter).

Hurst Trail →

Passes Fingerboard Shelter and leads 0.5 mile to Seven Lakes Drive at south end of Lake Tiorati. Named for Haven Hurst, a member of the Green Mountain Club who opened the trail in 1922.

N-S

| TRAIL DESCRIPTION |

0.0 The **northern end of section** is at Arden Valley Road, which leads east to **Tiorati Circle**. Southbound hikers proceed south onto a woods road where the red-on-white-blazed **Ramapo-Dunderberg (R-D) Trail** joins the A.T. from the east. Northbound hikers cross the road and reenter woods (New York Section Ten above).   **5.5**

0.1 Pass a round water tank to the east, at the foot of Fingerboard Mountain.   **5.4**

0.5 Summit of Fingerboard Mountain (elev. 1,328 ft.), marked by a stone fireplace to the right of Trail.   **5.0**

1.1 Blue-blazed **Hurst Trail** leads east 350 feet to **Fingerboard Shelter**, visible immediately below.   **4.4**

1.2 **Ramapo-Dunderberg (R-D) Trail** intersects the A.T. from the east, leading southward along the ridge. Southbound hikers follow A.T. to right and begin to descend, steeply in places. Northbound hikers follow A.T. and R-D trails north along ridge of Fingerboard Mountain.   **4.3**

Fire Closures—During very dry periods, some trails in Harriman State Park may be closed to the public to prevent forest fires; however, the A.T. should remain open under agreements with the Trail community. During such periods, hikers are advised to consult park staff members at the stone building just east of N.Y. 17 on Arden Valley Road or at the stone building at the Tiorati Circle for current information on the status of the trails in the park. For descriptions of the various trails crossing the A.T. in this section, as well as other trails in the vicinity, consult Harriman Trails: A Guide and History, *published by the New York–New Jersey Trail Conference.*

S-N

SECTION HIGHLIGHTS

Greenwood Mine →

Now a water-filled pit. Through the time of the Civil War, tens of thousands of tons of magnetite ore were conveyed by oxen and horse teams from this mine to Arden, home of the Greenwood charcoal furnace, built in 1811 by James Cunningham, and the Clove anthracite furnace, erected in 1854 by Robert and Peter Parrott. The pig iron was shipped by rail to Cornwall-on-Hudson, where it was ferried to the West Point foundry at Cold Spring. There, it was made into the famous Parrott guns and shells, designed by the same brothers who operated the mines and furnaces. Surebridge Mine Road also leads to the Surebridge Mine and the Pine Swamp Mine south of the Trail.

Long Path →

A developing system that comprises more than 300 miles of footpaths and is maintained by the New York–New Jersey Trail Conference. The path was promoted in the 1930s by Raymond Torrey and developed beginning in the 1960s. Its main stem leads from the Palisades along the Hudson, through Harriman to Schunemunk Mountain, and then to the Shawangunks, Catskills, and parts north.

Lemon Squeezer →

A famous, steep, and sometimes claustrophobia-inducing passage between boulders. If too steep or narrow, use the bypass trail to the west.

Arden-Surebridge Trail →

Extends 6.3 miles between Old Arden Road (at intersection with A.T., at mile 5.0 below) and Seven Lakes Drive.

Island Pond →

The outlet is partially channeled into a spillway made of cut stones. This spillway was constructed by the CCC in 1934 as part of a plan to dam the pond and enlarge it. However, the work was never completed, and the pond remains in its natural state. A shelter built near the lake was removed in the 1970s when the Trail was relocated.

N-S

	TRAIL DESCRIPTION

1.7	Surebridge Mine Road briefly joins the A.T. at the foot of a steep incline, along Surebridge Brook, near **Greenwood Mine.**	3.8
1.8	Cross Surebridge Brook in the swampy hollow between Surebridge and Fingerboard mountains.	3.7
2.1	Reach high point on Surebridge Mountain (elev. 1,200 ft.).	3.4
2.4	A.T. crosses an intermittent stream between Surebridge and Island Pond mountains.	3.1
2.6	The aqua-blazed **Long Path** crosses the Trail.	2.9
3.0	Reach the summit of Island Pond Mountain (elev. 1,303 ft.).	2.5
3.2	Reach the **Lemon Squeezer**. Below the Lemon Squeezer, the **Arden-Surebridge (A-SB) Trail**, with red-triangle-on-white blazes, briefly joins the A.T. on the east side of the Trail.	2.3
3.5	A.T. briefly joins the Crooked Road, an old woods road, and crosses the inlet of Island Pond.	2.0
3.7	Reach the crest of a rise, with a view of Island Pond to the east.	1.8
3.8	Cross a bridge over the outlet of **Island Pond**.	1.7
3.9	Cross a gravel road, which provides automobile access (by permit only—leads west 0.3 mile to Arden Valley Road) for fishermen to Island Pond.	1.6
4.0	A woods road, Island Pond Road, built by Edward Harriman around 1905, briefly joins the A.T. at the foot of Green Pond Mountain.	1.5
4.2	Reach the summit of Green Pond Mountain (elev. 1,180 ft.) with limited views from rocks to the west of the Trail.	1.3

S-N

Old Arden Road →

This woods road once connected the Arden estate of the Harriman family with the community of Tuxedo; the road was partially destroyed by the construction of the New York State Thruway. During the Civil War, Arden was a booming mining town, with a population of more than 2,000. But smelting with coal soon replaced smelting with charcoal, and the iron deposits of Pennsylvania and the Great Lakes region were found much easier to mine (although not of as high a quality). By 1890, the mining industry in this area had all but disappeared.

Elk Pen parking area →

The field to the east of this parking area, with pieces of metal fence, is all that remains of an unsuccessful attempt by the park to establish an elk herd here.

New York State Thruway →

I-87 extends 346 miles from New York City to Champlain, New York. The Thruway system, which also includes portions of Interstates 84, 90, and 287, comprises 641 miles of highway.

Southern end of section →

Drivers approaching this end of the Trail *via* the New York Thruway should note that the closest exits onto N.Y. 17 are at Harriman to the north (exit 16) and Sloatsburg/Suffern to the south (exit 15A). From New York City and local points to the north, Short Line Bus System, (201) 444-7005, will stop on request at the junction of N.Y. 17 and Arden Valley Road. Scheduled stops are made at the Red Apple Rest in Southfields, 2.1 miles to the south on N.Y. 17. Restaurants and a motel are located in Southfields, and a deli, with groceries, is 1.8 miles south of the crossing. The nearest post office is at Arden (ZIP Code 10910), 0.7 mile north on N.Y. 17. (The post office is located in the former Arden railroad station, 0.2 mile east of N.Y. 17 on a secondary road.) A post office is also at Southfields (ZIP Code 10975). A larger selection of groceries is in Tuxedo, 5.7 miles to the south on N.Y. 17.

N-S

	TRAIL DESCRIPTION	

4.4 The Trail switches back across the slope of Green Pond   **1.1**
Mountain.

5.0 The Trail intersects with **Old Arden Road** at the foot of   **0.5**
Green Pond Mountain. Southbound hikers turn right and
follow the road. Northbound hikers turn left, enter the
woods, and begin a steady ascent of Green Pond Mountain. The Arden-Surebridge Trail (red-triangle-on-white
blazes) intersects in 100 feet.

5.1 The Trail intersects with paved Arden Valley Road. South-   **0.4**
bound hikers turn left and follow the road. Northbound
hikers bear right and follow unpaved Old Arden Road.

5.2 Pass the entrance to **Elk Pen parking area** on the south   **0.3**
side of the road.

5.3 Cross **New York State Thruway**, Ramapo River, and rail-   **0.2**
road tracks on overpass.

5.5 Reach the **southern end of section** at N.Y. 17. Southbound   **0.0**
hikers continue across road and reenter woods (New York
Section Twelve below). Northbound hikers follow blazes
along Arden Valley Road.

S-N

N.Y. 17 (Arden)
to N.Y. 17A (Mt. Peter)

12.0 MILES

The A.T. traverses four low mountains across this section—Arden Mountain, Buchanan Mountain, Mombasha High Point, and Bellvale Mountain—and runs through the northern section of Sterling Forest, a 20,000-acre tract that includes the sites of many former iron mines and of the Sterling Furnace, which supplied a famous chain that stretched across the Hudson River near West Point during the Revolutionary War.

The elevation at N.Y. 17 is 500 feet. At N.Y. 17A, the elevation is 1,130 feet. The highest elevation is 1,294 feet on Bellvale Mountain.

Both the northern and southern ends of this section are accessible by vehicle. Road access is also available at Orange Turnpike (mile 1.8 below), East Mombasha Road (mile 3.2 below), West Mombasha Road (mile 4.9 below), and Lakes Road (mile 8.4 below). No parking is available at Orange Turnpike or West Mombasha Road. Limited parking is available at East Mombasha Road and Lakes Road, but overnight parking is not permitted.

Maps—For route navigation, refer to Map 3 with this guide. For area detail, refer to the following USGS 7½-minute topographic quadrangles: Monroe, New York; Warwick, New York; Greenwood Lake, New York–New Jersey.

Shelters and Campsites—This section has one shelter, Wildcat Shelter, at mile 9.9 below. Camping is not permitted elsewhere in the section. Campfires are permitted only at the fire ring at Wildcat Shelter.

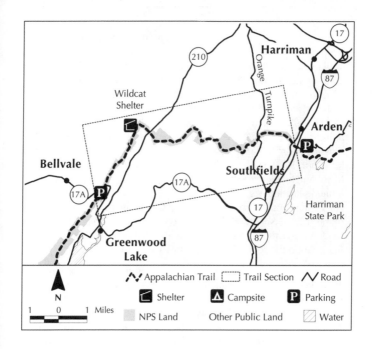

Appalachian Trail · Trail Section · Road
Shelter · Campsite · Parking
NPS Land · Other Public Land · Water

1 0 1 Miles

N

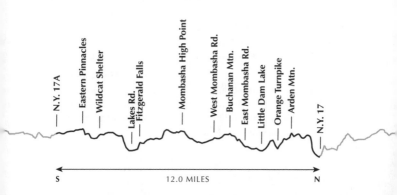

N.Y. 17A
Eastern Pinnacles
Wildcat Shelter
Lakes Rd.
Fitzgerald Falls
Mombasha High Point
West Mombasha Rd.
Buchanan Mtn.
East Mombasha Rd.
Little Dam Lake
Orange Turnpike
Arden Mtn.
N.Y. 17

S — 12.0 MILES — N

Northern end of section →

No parking is available at the Trail crossing, but ample parking is available at the Elk Pen parking area on Arden Valley Road, 0.3 mile north of the crossing (New York Section Eleven above). The closest New York State Thruway exits are at Harriman to the north (exit 16) and Sloatsburg/Suffern to the south (exit 15A). Short Line Bus System, (201) 444-7005, provides connections from New York City and local points to the north. A flag stop will be made on request at the Trail crossing at Arden Valley Road, and scheduled stops are made at the Red Apple Rest in Southfields, 2.1 miles south of the A.T. on N.Y. 17. Meals and lodging may be obtained in Southfields, and a deli, with a limited selection of groceries, is 1.8 miles south of the Trail crossing. The nearest post office is at Arden (ZIP Code 10910), 0.7 mile north of the A.T. on N.Y. 17 and 0.2 mile east of N.Y. 17 on a secondary road. A post office is also at Southfields (ZIP Code 10975); Tuxedo, 5.5 miles to the south on N.Y. 17, has a supermarket.

Ramapo River Valley →

The hiker will encounter many Indian names in this area. Ramapo means "formed of round ponds," used to denote a river in which potholes occur. "Tuxedo" is a word that may have been derived from *P'tauk-seet-tough,* which means "the place of bears," though it may have come instead from "Duck Cedar," a name found on old maps of the area. Although many area lakes have Indian names, those lakes are, in fact, man-made and have no connection with the tribes that once inhabited the Hudson Highlands. The community of Tuxedo Park, east of here, was long a retreat for Manhattan's richest families and birthplace of the "tuxedo" dinner jacket.

Catskill Mountains →

The Catskills, northwest of the A.T. and west of the Hudson River above Kingston, New York, are one of New York's most scenic areas, and their streams and lakes feed reservoirs and aqueducts that provide drinking water for New York City.

N-S

TRAIL DESCRIPTION

0.0 The **northern end of section** is at the intersection of N.Y. 17 and Arden Valley Road. Southbound hikers follow blazes compass-west, entering woods on footpath and beginning steep 500-foot climb of "Agony Grind." Northbound hikers follow Arden Valley Road over New York State Thruway (New York Section Eleven above). **12.0**

0.4 Reach viewpoint (above "Agony Grind") to east over **Ramapo River Valley** and New York State Thruway, with Harriman State Park beyond. **11.6**

0.7 A blue-blazed trail intersects on the east side of the A.T. (compass-south) and leads 0.4 mile to the yellow-blazed Indian Hill Loop Trail in Sterling Forest State Park. **11.3**

0.8 Pass Trail register (please sign) located on tree to east of Trail. **11.2**

1.1 Reach scrub-oak-covered summit of Arden Mountain (elev. 1,180 ft.), with limited views west and north. **10.9**

1.5 Reach secondary peak, with views to west. **10.5**

1.6 Rocky ledges on ridge of Arden Mountain afford views west to Mombasha High Point and Bellvale Mountain and north to the **Catskill Mountains** on the horizon. **10.4**

S-N

SECTION HIGHLIGHTS

Orange Turnpike →

Originally a stagecoach route leading upstate through the "Ramapo Pass," one of the gaps in the Highlands. A piped spring, a water source, is 0.5 mile south of the Trail crossing on the east side of road, by a gravel pull-off area beyond a dip in road. No parking.

Sterling Forest →

Named for Lord Stirling, a Revolutionary War general of Scottish origin, who fought in the battle of Long Island and other battles but died at Albany from natural causes before the war ended. His original name was William Alexander, and he never officially received the title he claimed. The Harriman family bought Sterling Forest in the late 1800s and offered the land to New York State for park purposes in the early 1950s. The state declined, claiming that it contained too many wetlands and other problem areas and asserting that New York already had sufficient parklands to provide for future needs. As a result, the Harriman family sold the land to private interests. During the 1970s, the National Park Service acquired a narrow corridor through which the Trail presently runs. In the mid-1980s, the new owners of Sterling Forest announced plans to develop it, and concerned citizens began extensive efforts to preserve the property in its natural state. As a result, Passaic County, New Jersey, condemned the 2,100 acres of Sterling Forest located in New Jersey to acquire them as watershed lands, and the National Park Service acquired additional lands to buffer the A.T. around Little Dam Lake. The New York–New Jersey Trail Conference, ATC, and many other conservation and environmental organizations joined with the Palisades Interstate Park Commission and the states of New York and New Jersey to form the Public/Private Partnership to Save Sterling Forest to preserve the remainder of this important natural resource. The result of this effort is the new Sterling Forest State Park, which now comprises18,000 acres of forests, lakes, streams, and other sensitive natural resources, traversed by numerous hiking trails—a key part of the Appalachian Greenway.

N-S

TRAIL DESCRIPTION

Little Dam Lake

1.8 Reach paved **Orange Turnpike** in a hollow between hills. **10.2**
The Trail turns left and follows the road for 250 feet, then
turns right and reenters the woods.

2.1 Pass a viewpoint to east, above hemlock grove. **9.9**

2.5 Eastern end of Little Dam Lake in **Sterling Forest**. South- **9.5**
bound hikers pass around northern side of lake, which
is visible to left of Trail. Northbound hikers begin ascent
through hemlock grove.

2.9 Cross wood-truss bridge over inlet of Little Dam Lake. **9.1**

3.2 Cross paved East Mombasha Road. **8.8**

3.4 Reach a viewpoint to the east over Little Dam Lake at a **8.6**
secondary summit of Buchanan Mountain.

3.6 Cross a series of four streams on the slopes below Bu- **8.4**
chanan Mountain.

S-N

SECTION HIGHLIGHTS

West Mombasha Road →

Sandwiches, limited supplies, and a pay phone are available at a deli 0.6 mile west (compass-north) along West Mombasha Road. The overgrown field along the Trail to the west of the road has been designated as a butterfly refuge. No parking.

Mombasha High Point →

The view from this rocky outcrop is to the south, over Indian Kill Reservoir and the hills of Sterling Forest State Park. There are limited views through the trees over Mombasha Lake from the Trail just north of Mombasha High Point. On clear days, the Manhattan skyline may be visible in the distance to the south.

Allis Trail →

This 2.5-mile trail is named for banker J. Ashton Allis, a pioneer Trail builder, for many years president of the Fresh Air Club, and an early treasurer of ATC. A viewpoint is located 100 feet down Allis Trail; High Point Monument and relay towers and Mt. Tammany at Delaware Water Gap may be visible to the west in clear conditions. Parking is available near the trailhead of the Allis Trail on N.Y. 17A.

Abandoned settlement →

In addition to old stone walls and roads, hikers in Sterling Forest and the Highlands may notice interesting circular depressions on the forest floor. Those are the remains of burning pits where wood was converted to charcoal needed for the smelting of iron ore. During the 1800s, the hills in this area were virtually denuded of vegetation as a result of harvesting the timber needed to produce the charcoal. The forest the hiker sees today is mostly secondary growth. Brooks and streams in the area are often colored brown as a result of iron salts leaching through the soil.

N-S	TRAIL DESCRIPTION	
4.0	Reach a beautiful viewpoint near the summit of Buchanan Mountain (elev. 1,142 ft.).	**8.0**
4.2	The Trail runs along the edge of an escarpment.	**7.8**
4.3	Cross jumbled rocks on a very steep section of Trail.	**7.7**
4.5	Cross a stream to the north of a hemlock grove and mountain-laurel thicket.	**7.5**
4.8	Cross a stream (outlet of a pond) south of a rocky section.	**7.2**
4.9	Cross paved **West Mombasha Road**.	**7.1**
5.0	Proceed across overgrown field and maple swamp on puncheon, passing a small pond to the west of the Trail.	**7.0**
5.4	Cross a grassy woods road.	**6.6**
5.7	Pass through a gap in a stone wall. Southbound hikers bear left at a fork just beyond the stone wall and begin a steady ascent. Northbound hikers bear right at two forks just beyond the stone wall.	**6.3**
6.1	Reach **Mombasha High Point** (elev. 1,280 ft.). Southbound hikers continue along the ridge. Northbound hikers descend *via* switchbacks.	**5.9**
6.9	Blue-blazed **Allis Trail** branches off to east and descends over One Cedar Mountain to N.Y. 17A. The teal-blazed Highlands Trail joins the A.T. and runs concurrently with it southward for 2.1 miles.	**5.1**
7.7	Pass old stone walls, remains of an **abandoned settlement**, to the east of the Trail.	**4.3**
7.9	Cross a dirt road.	**4.1**
8.0	Cross Trout Brook and a tributary.	**4.0**

S-N

SECTION HIGHLIGHTS

Cat Rocks

Wildcat Shelter →
Built in 1992 by local volunteers; accommodates 8; a privy, a cast-iron fire ring, and three tent sites are also available. Water may be obtained from a spring. Next shelter: north, 14.3 miles (Fingerboard Shelter); south, 12.0 miles (Wawayanda Shelter).

Cat Rocks →
A popular "bouldering" spot for rock climbers. It is a good place to see the effects of Ice Age glaciers on the landscape. According to A.T. geologist V. Collins Chew, it is part of the same ridge of rock that hikers follow along Bearfort and Bellvale Mountains, farther south, its red "puddingstone" rocks having been "smoothed and rounded by the grit carried across it by ice sheets. Some of these open ledges provide good views of Greenwood Lake [page 141 below], which lies along the eroded fault line marking the eastern boundary of this area…. White-quartz veins are common, and polished slickensides trace the course of rock scraping against each other during faulting. The tremendous pressure smeared the white and red pebbles in places" (*Underfoot: A Geologic Guide to the Appalachian Trail*).

N-S

TRAIL DESCRIPTION

8.1	Pass Fitzgerald Falls, a 25-foot waterfall in a rocky cleft. At the base of falls, southbound hikers turn right, crossing the brook, and continue along the brook. A blue-blazed bypass trail to the east leads south, rejoining the A.T. at mile 8.2 below, avoiding two crossings of the brook and a frequently flooded area. Northbound hikers ascend the east side of falls along Trout Brook.	**3.9**
8.2	Blue-blazed bypass trail to the east leads north, avoiding two additional crossings of Trout Brook, and rejoining the A.T. at mile 8.1 above.	**3.8**
8.3	Cross a wooden bridge over Trout Brook.	**3.7**
8.4	Cross paved Lakes Road (Monroe Road). Southbound hikers cross the road and soon begin to ascend Bellvale Mountain. Northbound hikers descend to the bridge over Trout Brook.	**3.6**
8.8	The Trail turns sharply above a steep section on Bellvale Mountain.	**3.2**
9.0	The teal-blazed Highlands Trail intersects on the west side of the A.T. and runs concurrently with A.T. to the north for 2.1 miles, to the Allis Trail. Northbound hikers follow an old woods road (now merely a footpath) along the ridge.	**3.0**
9.7	Cross an old stone wall.	**2.3**
9.9	A blue-blazed trail to the west leads 600 feet to **Wildcat Shelter**, just north of a small brook crossing.	**2.1**
10.2	The Trail crosses **Cat Rocks**, with views to the east and south. A short blue-blazed trail bypasses a steep section.	**1.8**
10.4	Cross a brook.	**1.6**

S-N

Greenwood Lake →

A nine-mile-long lake, called Long Pond before it was dammed and enlarged in the nineteenth century to provide water for the nearby Morris Canal, it extends on both sides of the New York–New Jersey border. The resort village on the east side of the lake has a selection of stores and restaurants; bus service is available.

Southern end of section →

Parking is available on the paved strip of the old highway (known as Continental Road). The crossing can be reached from New York City and from Warwick, New York, by New Jersey Transit buses, (973) 762-5100. A flag stop will be made on request at Mt. Peter (Kain Road), 0.2 mile west of the A.T. on N.Y. 17A. A grocery store and post office (ZIP Code 10912) are in Bellvale, 1.6 miles west of the A.T. on N.Y. 17A. A variety of supplies and services, including restaurants, a supermarket, tourist homes, and a post office (ZIP Code 10925) are available at Greenwood Lake, 2.0 miles south of the A.T. on N.Y. 17A and N.Y. 210. Motels are available in Warwick, 3.5 miles to the west along N.Y. 17A.

N-S

| TRAIL DESCRIPTION |

10.6 Cross an open, rocky area.

10.7 Reach the top of Eastern Pinnacles, a conglomerate out-cropping, with good views to the north, east, and south over **Greenwood Lake**. A short blue-blazed trail to the west bypasses a steep section.

11.3 Cross a cleared utility right-of-way.

11.6 A woods road intersects with the A.T. from the west.

11.9 A blue-blazed side trail intersects on the west side of the A.T. and leads 0.2 mile to a hawk watch platform, with limited views.

12.0 Reach N.Y. 17A. At the crossing, southbound hikers turn right and follow road for 150 feet, then take left fork onto an old road (Continental Road). Continue on Continental Road for 150 feet until the Trail turns left and reenters the woods on a footpath (**southern end of section**; see New York Section Thirteen). Northbound hikers proceed east along Continental Road for 150 feet to its intersection with N.Y. 17A, then cross to northern side of N.Y. 17A. Turn right, and follow road for 150 feet, then turn left, and enter the woods on footpath.

S-N

N.Y. 17A (Mt. Peter) to New York–New Jersey State Line

5.9 MILES

The Trail follows the ridge of Bellvale Mountain (called Bearfort Mountain in New Jersey) and offers many beautiful views over Greenwood Lake and the Ramapo Hills from open ledges. Although the elevation changes little between the northern and southern ends of the section, the route is not easy, with many short, steep ascents and descents along the crest of a rocky, glacier-scarred ridge. The highest point is at Prospect Rock (elev. 1,433 ft.). The Trail passes through oak and hickory forests, with pitch pine on the rocky ledges.

Road Approaches—Only the northern end of the section is directly accessible by car. The southern end of the section is at the New York-New Jersey state boundary, atop the ridge. The nearest authorized road access to this point is from N.Y. 210, which runs along the shore of Greenwood Lake, *via* the State Line Trail.

Maps—For route navigation, refer to Maps 3 and 4 with this guide. For area detail, refer to the following USGS 7½-minute topographic quadrangle: Greenwood Lake, New York–New Jersey. Another reference is NY–NJ TC North Jersey Trails Map 21.

Shelters and Campsites—No shelters or campsites are available in this section. Camping and campfires are not permitted.

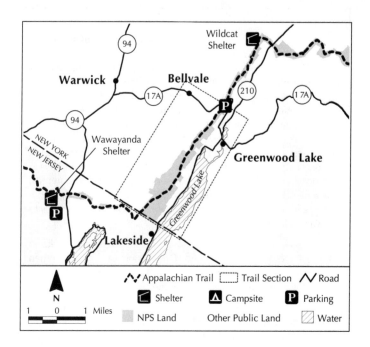

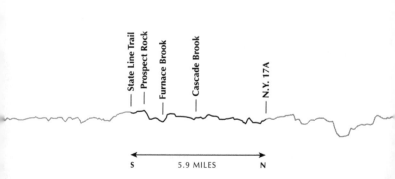

SECTION HIGHLIGHTS

Northern end of section →

The Trail crosses N.Y. 17A two miles north of the village of Greenwood Lake and 1.6 miles east of Bellvale. This end of the section starts at Continental Road, the paved strip of the old highway around which improved N.Y. 17A has been built. Ample parking is available along Continental Road at the Trail crossing. Public transportation is available from New York City and from Warwick, New York (by New Jersey Transit buses (973) 762-5100). A flag stop will be made on request at Mt. Peter (Kain Road), 0.2 mile west of the Trail crossing on N.Y. 17A. A grocery store and post office (ZIP Code 10912) are located at Bellvale. Supplies and services, including restaurants, convenience stores, and a post office (ZIP Code 10925) are available in Greenwood Lake. Motels are available in Warwick, 3.5 miles to the west, along N.Y. 17A.

Greenwood Lake →

Originally known as Long Pond, Greenwood Lake was dammed to increase its size, first in the 1760s and again in the early 1800s, when it served as a water source for the Morris Canal.

Bellvale Mountain →

Streams flowing from Bellvale Mountain supplied water to furnaces and forges in the area. The Iron Act of 1750 sought to close iron forges in the American colonies, including one in nearby Bellvale, so they would depend on Britain's iron industry. The tilt-hammer iron forge at Bellvale, near the northern end of the section, was the only mill of its kind in the New York province. It was destroyed by English soldiers after the act passed, which led to an early American grievance against the British.

N-S

TRAIL DESCRIPTION

0.0   The **northern end of section** is on paved Continental Road, just south of N.Y. 17A near Mt. Peter. Southbound hikers enter the woods, cross a woods road, and ascend. Northbound hikers turn right and proceed along N.Y. 17A, which comes in from the left. Then, turn left, and enter woods (see New York Section Twelve, above).   **5.9**

0.5   Pass through a powerline clearing, with good views to the east. The summit of Mt. Peter (elev. 1,210 ft.) is to the west.   **5.4**

0.8   Under telephone lines, cross a brook, the outlet of a marsh to the west of the Trail.   **5.1**

2.0   The blue-blazed Village Vista Trail, open Spring 2003, intersects on the east side of the A.T., leads downhill 0.8 mile to the village of Greenwood Lake.   **3.9**

2.2   Emerge onto an exposed section of the ridge, with beautiful views of **Greenwood Lake** to the east.   **3.7**

2.5   Cross a small brook below a steep section.   **3.4**

2.9   Cross Cascade Brook, between a cleared area and a hemlock grove.   **3.0**

3.1   Pass a viewpoint atop **Bellvale Mountain**.   **2.8**

View of Greenwood Lake

S-N

SECTION HIGHLIGHTS

Cascade Lake Park →

Acquired by the town of Warwick in 1998, with assistance from the ATC Land Trust, the New York–New Jersey Trail Conference, the Trust for Public Land, and local donations. Parking is available at the entrance to the park, about 1.1 miles from the A.T.

Prospect Rock →

The "puddingstone" here, some 350 million or more years old, is a conglomerate of red and white quartz pebbles, and pebbles and chips of other rock types, and shows the scraping action of glaciers.

State Line Trail →

Descends from the A.T. and follows the New York–New Jersey state line to N.Y. 210. From its junction with the A.T. at the southern end of this section, it proceeds east and crosses the ridge of Bellvale Mountain, with numerous short ascents and descents. At 0.4 mile, the State Line Trail starts a steady descent. The yellow-blazed Ernest Walter Trail, which makes a loop around Surprise Lake and West Pond, turns off to the right at 0.5 mile. With houses in view to the right at 0.9 mile, the State Line Trail turns left and continues its descent until it reaches N.Y. 210, opposite the Greenwood Lake Marina, at 1.2 miles.

Southern end of section →

Not accessible by car. Limited parking is available at the trailhead of the State Line Trail, just south of the intersection of N.Y. 210 with Lake Shore Road. The parking area is on the west side of the road (do not park at the marina on the east side of the road). Public transportation is available *via* New Jersey Transit buses. Restaurants and convenience stores are located at the intersection of Lakeside Road (the continuation in New Jersey of N.Y. 210) with Greenwood Lake Turnpike, 2.5 miles south of the trailhead. A supermarket and the Hewitt, New Jersey post office (ZIP Code 07421) are in a shopping center just west of this intersection.

N-S	TRAIL DESCRIPTION	
3.3	Cross a brook several times.	2.6
3.4	Cross open rocks, with good views to the east over Greenwood Lake.	2.5
3.9	Reach a rock outcropping that offers a 360-degree view.	2.0
4.3	Cross an old road to the south of a very steep section.	1.6
4.5	Cross Furnace Brook, a water source.	1.4
5.3	Pass a rocky promontory to the west, just south of a steep section. The promontory offers good views to the west, north, and east.	0.6
5.4	The blue-blazed Zig Zag Trail, which intersects on the west side of the A.T., leads to **Cascade Lake Park.**	0.5
5.5	Reach **Prospect Rock** (elev. 1,433 ft.), an outcropping of "puddingstone," with views over Greenwood Lake to the east and Taylor and Warwick mountains to the west. New York City's skyline may be visible beyond ridges to east.	0.4
5.8	Pass a Trail register (please sign) located on a pine tree to the east of the Trail.	0.1
5.9	Reach the blue-blazed **State Line Trail** on the east side of the A.T. at the New York–New Jersey state line (**southern end of section**). Southbound hikers continue ahead (see New Jersey Section One, below). Northbound hikers proceed north on footpath.	0.0

New Jersey

Although New Jersey is generally thought of as urban, full of industrial towns, busy highways, and bedroom communities, the Appalachian Trail reveals to hikers a different side of the state—one that is quite remote and wild in its character.

The southern part of the Trail in New Jersey follows the ridge of

Kittatinny Mountain, southeast of the Delaware River, through broad expanses of state forest and national-recreation-area land that teem with mountain flora and fauna—including a healthy population of black bears. Northeast of High Point, the Trail changes direction sharply, and runs along the New York–New Jersey line, between the "Skylands" of Kittatinny Ridge and the Highlands of Pochuck and Wawayanda mountains. The valleys in between reveal a varied landscape of farms, forests, suburbs, grassy wetlands, abandoned iron mines, wooded swamps, and old railroad grades. If you have preconceptions about New Jersey, a hike on the Appalachian Trail may change your mind.

New York–New Jersey State Line to N.J. 94

9.3 MILES

The northern end of this section of Trail is at the New York–New Jersey state line along the ridge of Bearfort Mountain, west of Greenwood Lake. South of there, it follows the ridge, passing through Abram S. Hewitt State Forest, then turns west and begins to run in a generally northwesterly direction, parallel to the state line. It crosses Warwick Turnpike and traverses Wawayanda State Park, passing through an upland deciduous forest, with some red cedar, hemlock, and rhododendron.

Only the southern end of this section is directly accessible by vehicle. The northern end of the section is at the New York–New Jersey state boundary; the nearest road access is 1.2 miles east, *via* the State Line Trail, from N.Y. 210 along the shore of Greenwood Lake. Road access is also available at Long House Road (Brady Road), mile 2.2 below, and at Warwick Turnpike, mile 3.6 below. Ample parking is available at the headquarters of Wawayanda State Park.

Maps—For route navigation, refer to Map 4 with this guide. For area detail, refer to the following USGS 7½-minute topographic quadrangles: Greenwood Lake, New York–New Jersey; Wawayanda, New Jersey–New York. Another reference is NY–NJ TC North Jersey Trails Map 21.

Shelters and Campsites—This section has one shelter, Wawayanda Shelter, at mile 4.0 below. Camping is not permitted elsewhere in the section, and campfires are not permitted.

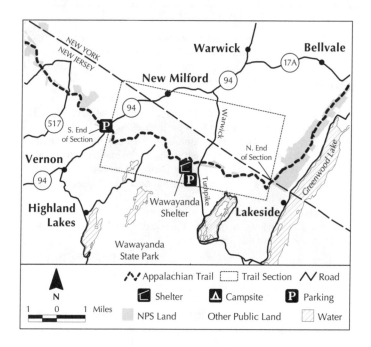

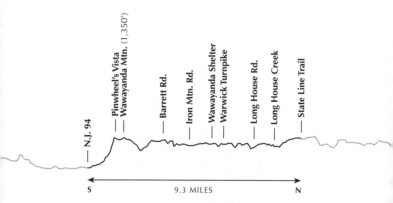

Note—Because of the east-west orientation of the Trail in this section, the "northern" end of the section is actually farther south than the "southern" end. See page 14 for an explanation of how compass directions are used in this guide.

Northern end of section →
Not accessible by car. Limited parking is available at the trailhead of the State Line Trail, just south of the intersection of N.Y. 210 with Lake Shore Road. The parking area is on the west side of the road (do not park at the marina on the east side of the road). Public transportation is available *via* New Jersey Transit buses. Restaurants and convenience stores are located at the intersection of Lakeside Road (the continuation in New Jersey of N.Y. 210) with Greenwood Lake Turnpike, 2.5 miles south of the trailhead. A supermarket and the Hewitt, New Jersey post office (ZIP Code 07421) are in a shopping center just west of this intersection.

State Line Trail →
Descends from the A.T. and follows the New York–New Jersey state line to N.Y. 210. From the A.T., it proceeds east down the ridge of Bellvale Mountain, with numerous short ascents and descents. At 0.4 mile, it turns sharply to the right, then immediately to the left, and starts a steady descent. The yellow-blazed Ernest Walter Trail, which makes a loop around Surprise Lake and West Pond, intersects on the right at 0.5 mile. With houses in view to the right at 0.9 mile, the State Line Trail turns left and continues its descent until it reaches N.Y. 210, opposite the Greenwood Lake Marina, at 1.2 miles.

Abram S. Hewitt State Forest →
A 2,009-acre state forest atop Bearfort Mountain in Passaic County, New Jersey. It is named after a nineteenth-century iron magnate and New York City mayor who once owned the land.

Ernest Walter Trail →
Makes loop around West Pond and glacially formed Surprise Lake and connects in about 1.0 mile with the white-blazed Bearfort Ridge Trail, leading 2.5 miles south to Warwick Turnpike.

N-S

TRAIL DESCRIPTION

Surprise Lake in Abram S. Hewitt State Forest

0.0	The **northern end of section** is at the junction with the **State Line Trail** on Bearfort Mountain (called Bellvale Mountain in New York) in **Abram S. Hewitt State Forest**.	**9.3**
0.2	Reach a viewpoint looking east over Surprise Lake and Sterling Ridge.	**9.1**
0.3	The yellow-blazed **Ernest Walter Trail** intersects on the east side of the A.T., where it turns sharply.	**9.0**
0.5	Reach a rock ledge, with a view to the west.	**8.8**
0.7	Cross rocks over a small stream.	**8.6**
0.8	Cross a woods road. In 450 feet, cross another woods road.	**8.5**

S-N

Long House Road →

Leads east to a lakeside residential community along Upper Greenwood Lake, a man-made lake dammed early in the last century, and west onto Warwick Mountain.

Old woods road →

This section of the Trail, which passes the remnants of many old iron mines, crosses numerous old farm and woods roads that date back to the 1700s and 1800s, when the forests of Wawayanda Mountain were stripped to feed nearby furnaces.

Warwick Turnpike →

Ample parking is available at the headquarters of Wawayanda State Park, located about 0.3 mile south of the Trail crossing. Registration is required for overnight parking. A blue-blazed side trail (mile 3.9 below) links the headquarters with the A.T. A seasonal farm market and ice-cream stand is on Warwick Turnpike, 0.2 mile east of the Trail crossing, and meals are available at restaurants along Warwick Turnpike, both 0.8 mile west and 1.5 miles east of the Trail crossing. A supermarket is at the junction of N.Y. 94 and Warwick Turnpike, 2.7 miles west of the Trail. A deli, with groceries, is located on Warwick Turnpike, 1.8 miles east of the Trail. In addition, lodging may be obtained at a motel, 0.8 mile west of the Trail.

Wawayanda State Park →

A 13,422-acre state park surrounding Wawayanda Lake that includes swimming, camping, boating, and hiking facilities. *Wawayanda* is a Lenape Indian word for "winding waters." Wawayanda Mountain had been named by the time of the Revolutionary War; in 1846, the name was given to Wawayanda Lake, created from two natural ponds.

N-S

	TRAIL DESCRIPTION	

1.0	The Trail briefly follows a dirt road.	8.3
1.1	Cross a split-log bridge over Long House Creek.	8.2
1.5	Cross a wooden bridge over a stream.	7.8
1.7	The A.T. follows a woods road for a short distance.	7.6
1.9	The Trail follows a grassy woods road.	7.4
2.2	The Trail follows paved **Long House Road** (Brady Road) for a short distance, then crosses it.	7.1
2.3	The Trail crosses logs over an intermittent stream, near an old woods road at the border of Sussex and Passaic counties.	7.0
2.5	Negotiate a steep section under hemlock trees.	6.8
2.6	The Trail turns sharply.	6.7
2.9	Cross an **old woods road**.	6.4
3.1	Cross a brook.	6.2
3.3	Follow a farm road along an overgrown field just south of switchbacks on Maple Hill.	6.0
3.4	Follow a farm road along the edge of a field north of wooded sections.	5.9
3.5	Cross the remains of an old stone wall.	5.8
3.6	Cross paved **Warwick Turnpike**, the boundary of Wawayanda State Park.	5.7
3.8	Cross a plank bridge over a swamp outlet.	5.5
3.9	Join a woods road. A blue-blazed trail leads along the road east 0.3 mile to the headquarters of **Wawayanda State Park**.	5.4

S-N

SECTION HIGHLIGHTS

Wawayanda Shelter →

Built in 1990 by residents of Vernon Township with assistance from staff of Wawayanda State Park; accommodates 6; water is available at park headquarters, 0.4 mile from shelter (reached *via* another blue-blazed side trail). Fires are not permitted. An active bear population is in the area. Next shelter: north, 12.0 miles (Wildcat Shelter); south, 11.8 miles (Pochuck Mountain Shelter).

Wawayanda Road →

Leads east to Wawayanda Lake and west to N.Y. 94.

Iron Mountain Road →

Not passable by car. Leads west to N.Y. 94 and east to Wawayanda Lake.

 Puncheon (bog bridges)—Puncheon comes in several varieties. The simplest, most rustic, and most long-lived is the topped-log variety. Depending on the type of wood, its surface characteristics and the setting, the puncheon may get slippery. The big problem with split puncheon—hand-split, especially—is that all grain is open to water, it rots much faster, and it is weaker than topped-log puncheon.

Occasionally, puncheon sections must cross wetlands in which water may flood intermittently to depths of two to three feet. In those cases, maintainers replace the sill logs with small cribs, to raise the stringers above the annual flood stage. Where annual flood waters exceed a depth of three feet, as in New Jersey's Pochuck Quagmire, boardwalks have been built on both helical piers and piles, techniques that may become more important in the future on sections where the Appalachian Trail or its side trails must cross significant floodplains.

—Condensed from *Appalachian Trail Design, Construction and Maintenance,* by Robert D. Proudman and William Birchard.

N-S

TRAIL DESCRIPTION

4.0 A blue-blazed trail to the east leads 0.1 mile up a small   **5.3**
rise to **Wawayanda Shelter.**

4.3 The Trail follows dirt **Wawayanda Road** for 0.2 mile.   **5.0**

4.6 Reach the crest of a rise (elev. 1,210 ft.) on a woods road.   **4.7**

4.8 Pass a long-abandoned, overgrown field on the east side   **4.5**
of the Trail.

4.9 Trail intersects with dirt **Iron Mountain Road**. Southbound   **4.4**
hikers turn left and follow road past driveway (leads east to
stone foundations of the Kazmar house, built about 1815
and demolished in 1991). Northbound hikers turn right
off Iron Mountain Road onto grassy woods road.

5.1 Cross 1890s-era iron bridge over the Double Kill (stream).   **4.2**
Southbound hikers bear right at a fork and continue on
an old woods road. Northbound hikers follow dirt **Iron
Mountain Road** to the left.

5.5 Cross an intermittent stream.   **3.8**

5.6 Cross a wet area on puncheon.   **3.7**

5.7 Trail turns sharply. Southbound hikers turn left onto an   **3.6**
old woods road. Northbound hikers turn right, leaving
the woods road, and continue on a footpath.

5.9 Trail intersects with wide woods road. Southbound hik-   **3.4**
ers turn left and follow wide woods road between stone
walls. Northbound hikers turn right, leaving wide woods
road, and follow a narrower road.

S-N

SECTION HIGHLIGHTS

High Breeze Farm →

Also known as the Barrett Farm, one of the last intact nineteenth-century highland farms in New Jersey. It is now part of Wawayanda State Park and listed in the state and national registers of historic places. The farm is being restored.

Barrett Road →

A deli and post office (ZIP Code 10959) are in New Milford, New York, 1.8 miles west (compass-north) of Barrett Road (go north on Barrett Road for 1.6 miles, then turn right, and follow N.Y. 94 for 0.2 mile to Ryerson Road).

Luthers Rock →

This boulder is a glacial erratic, left behind by retreating ice sheets about 15,000 years ago.

Wawayanda Mountain →

A dramatic ridge that exhibits some of the oldest rock of the Appalachians—billion-year-old slabs of banded gneiss and other crystalline rocks formed during the Grenville Orogeny, at a time when the most advanced life on Earth was probably algae. The mountain was an important source of iron ore for eighteenth- and nineteenth-century mines and forges in the nearby Vernon Valley.

Wawayanda Ridge Trail →

Leads 0.8 mile to a viewpoint over the Vernon Valley and Pochuck Mountain.

Pinwheel's Vista →

"Pinwheel" was the nickname of a local Trail maintainer, Paul De-Coste. The vista offers spectacular views of the Shawangunks and Catskills, to compass-north, and Vernon Valley, Pochuck Mountain, and the Kittatinny Ridge to the west and south.

N-S   TRAIL DESCRIPTION

6.0 Cross a drain. Southbound hikers continue along a wide   **3.3**
         woods road, with an open field (**High Breeze Farm**) to the
         right. Northbound hikers begin to ascend.

6.2 The Trail crosses paved **Barrett Road** diagonally to the   **3.1**
         right. Southbound hikers climb wooden steps and enter a
         field. Northbound hikers climb stone steps, cross a stream,
         and continue along a wide woods road.

6.6 At top of ascent, pass **Luthers Rock**, with limited view to **2.7**
         the west through trees.

7.0 After descent, cross stream on wooden foot bridge.   **2.3**

7.4 Cross old woods road.   **1.9**

7.5 Cross two stone walls in succession below the crest of   **1.8**
         Wawayanda Mountain.

7.9 Reach high point (elev. 1,350 ft.) at the crest of **Wawa-** **1.4**
         yanda Mountain. The blue-blazed **Wawayanda Ridge**
         Trail intersects to the east, near a Trail register (please
         sign) on a tree.

8.0 Blue-blazed side trail intersects on the west side of the   **1.3**
         A.T. (leads 0.1 mile to **Pinwheel's Vista**), just above a
         long series of stone steps along the cliff of Wawayanda
         Mountain.

8.3 Trail reaches its southernmost point along Wawayanda   **1.0**
         Mountain and switches back.

Vernon Valley →

At the beginning of the last century, fewer people lived in this valley than had lived there in the colonial period, a fact that reflected the collapse of the iron-mining industry in the area. Later in the century, some of the valley's fruit and dairy farms began giving way to residential and vacation communities, and its population grew rapidly.

Southern end of section →

At N.J. 94, about 0.6 mile north of the intersection of N.J. 94 and Maple Grange Road and about 2.4 miles north of Vernon. A designated parking area is at the Trail crossing. No public transportation is available. The Appalachian Motel is located along N.J. 94, 1.4 miles east of the Trail crossing, and a seasonal farm market is 0.1 mile to the west along N.J. 94. A shopping center, with a 24-hour supermarket, a pizzeria, a deli, restaurants, and a post office (ZIP Code 07462), is in Vernon, 2.4 miles east (compass-south) of the Trail crossing along N.J. 94 and County 515.

N-S

TRAIL DESCRIPTION

8.6	Pass Annie's Bluff, above two small switchbacks and stone steps.	**0.7**
8.8	Reach the base (elev. 550 ft.) of the steep escarpment of **Wawayanda Mountain**.	**0.5**
8.9	Cross old stone wall above a field, with views of **Vernon Valley** and Pochuck Mountain.	**0.4**
9.1	Cross a gravel quarry road.	**0.2**
9.3	Reach N.J. 94 (**southern end of section**). Southbound hikers proceed straight across N.J. 94 into a field. Northbound hikers pass through an A.T. parking area and ascend a grassy path between stone drains.	**0.0**

S-N

N.J. 94 to N.J. 284
(Unionville, New York)

10.8 MILES

The Trail in this section cuts across the New Jersey's "drowned lands," running generally east to west along the New York–New Jersey line on a narrow corridor of land that passes through residential and farming communities and wildlife preserves. It passes through the swamps of Vernon Valley over a new boardwalk and bridge, then follows woods roads and paths over Pochuck Mountain. It runs along dikes on its way through a wildlife refuge that was formerly a sod farm, briefly follows a paved road across the Wallkill River, and continues through woods and farms. Few dependable sources of potable water are available along this section, and much of the water in the valleys is polluted, so plan to bring sufficient supplies.

Road Approaches—Both the northern and southern ends of this section are accessible by vehicle, and this section of Trail crosses more than half a dozen roads. Parking is available at several locations and at both ends.

Maps—For route navigation, refer to Map 4 of this guide. For area detail, refer to the following USGS 7½-minute topographic quadrangles: Wawayanda, New Jersey–New York; Hamburg, New Jersey; Unionville, New York–New Jersey.

Shelters and Campsites—This section has one shelter, Pochuck Mountain Shelter, at mile 6.5 below. Camping is not permitted except in the immediate vicinity of the shelter. An active bear population in the area makes it vital to take proper precautions when storing food overnight.

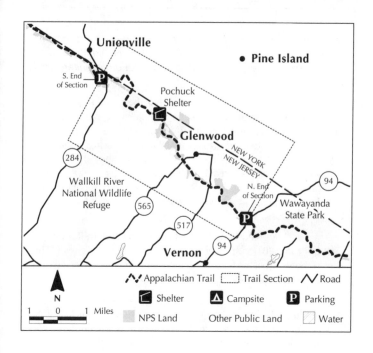

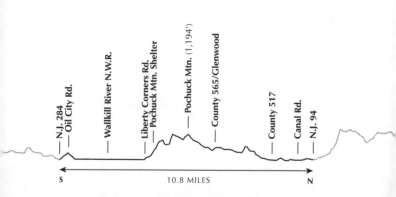

Note—*Because of the orientation of the Trail here, the "northern" end of the section is actually farther south than the "southern" end. See page 14 for an explanation of how compass directions are used in this guide.*

Northern end of section →

About 0.6 mile north of the intersection of N.J. 94 and Maple Grange Road and about 2.4 miles north of Vernon, New Jersey (ZIP Code 07462). A designated parking area is at the Trail crossing. A seasonal farm market is 0.1 mile to the west (compass-northeast) along N.J. 94, and a shopping center, with a supermarket, restaurants, and post office, is in Vernon, 2.4 miles east (compass-south) of the Trail crossing along N.J. 94 and County 515. A motel is 1.4 miles east of the Trail crossing.

New York, Susquehanna and Western Railway →

First built in 1881 as the Lehigh and Hudson River Railway. The route is now part of the NYS&W, which hauls freight between North Bergen, New Jersey, and Syracuse, New York.

Wawayanda Creek →

Archaeological digs in the Wawayanda ("winding waters") area around Vernon, New Jersey, and Wawayanda Mountain have produced evidence of many native American settlements.

Canal Road →

A short rural road. The large stream east of the A.T. is the canal itself, dug in the mid-nineteenth century to help drain the meadows of the Vernon Valley. The lowlands here and in the Wallkill Valley were known to the Dutch settlers as the "drowned lands," because of floods that regularly inundated them, making the rich soil hard to farm. Geologically, the swamps are the product of the last Ice Age, when glacial activity left rich deposits of sediments in the valleys at the foot of ridges scraped nearly barren by the ice.

N-S

| TRAIL DESCRIPTION |

0.0	The **northern end of section** is at the Trail crossing of N.J. 94. Southbound hikers proceed west from N.J. 94 and cross a cow pasture on puncheon (bog bridges). Northbound hikers proceed east from N.J. 94 and cross the hikers' parking area.	**10.8**
0.2	Cross over the **New York, Susquehanna and Western Railway** railroad tracks, using stiles on either side.	**10.6**
0.5	Pass through fields.	**10.3**
0.7	Cross bridge over **Wawayanda Creek**.	**10.1**
0.9	The A.T. intersects with **Canal Road**. Southbound hikers turn right along the road and cross a bridge over a creek. Northbound hikers turn left, leaving the road, and cross a field.	**9.9**
1.0	The A.T. intersects with **Canal Road**. Southbound hikers turn left, leaving the road, follow a woods road for 25 feet, then bear right onto a footpath. Northbound hikers turn right and follow the road across a bridge over a creek.	**9.8**

Pochuck Creek Bridge

S-N

Pochuck Swamp →

Also known as the "Pochuck Quagmire." In 2002, the New York–New Jersey Trail Conference and Appalachian Trail Conference opened the boardwalk and bridge over the nearly mile-wide swamp area—one of the most complicated and expensive construction projects in A.T. history and one that took more than seven years to complete. The relocation eliminates a long walk on roads through the Vernon Valley. The boardwalk was built on thin pilings bored deep into the swampy ground and was designed to permit passage of water even during periodic waist-deep floods.

Suspension bridge →

The 146-foot Pochuck Creek Bridge was completed in 1996, at a cost of $30,000, not including thousands of volunteer hours. Because of changing water levels in the area, its foundation essentially "floats." The walkway is 14 feet high, which is five feet above the 100-year flood level, and should permit the bridge to withstand floods that send logs and debris down the creek.

County 565 →

The community of Glenwood, New Jersey, is 0.7 mile west (compass-northeast), with a post office (ZIP Code 07418) and groceries. The Apple Valley Inn, a historic farmhouse, is one mile west of the Trail crossing. No public transportation is available. Near the A.T. crossing is the former Glenwood School, built in 1864 and used until 1958. The headquarters and visitor center for the Wallkill River National Wildlife Center is 5.0 miles east (compass-south), at 1547 County Route 565, in the town of Sussex.

Pochuck Mountain →

Though not high in comparison with other A.T. mountains, Pochuck Mountain is steep and dramatic—a formation of billion-year-old rock scraped nearly bare during the last Ice Age that juts out of the alluvial fields of the "drowned lands" (see mile 1.0 above).

N-S	TRAIL DESCRIPTION	
1.2	Reach the top of a knoll and begin to descend.	9.6
1.4	Cross a wooden bridge.	9.4
1.5	Cross an 850-foot-long stretch of boardwalk over **Pochuck Swamp**.	9.3
1.6	Cross a **suspension bridge** over Pochuck Creek.	9.2
1.7	Cross a 1,100-foot-long stretch of boardwalk over Pochuck Swamp.	9.1
2.1	Cross a 2,000-foot-long stretch of boardwalk over Pochuck Swamp.	8.7
2.3	The A.T. intersects with County 517 below the eastern face of Pochuck Mountain. Southbound hikers cross the road and turn right, briefly paralleling the road, then ascend. Northbound hikers continue ahead on a boardwalk over **Pochuck Swamp**.	8.5
2.9	After a steady ascent, reach the top of a rise and begin to descend.	7.9
3.8	Cross **County 565**, near the old Glenwood School building.	7.0
3.9	Cross wooden bridge over a stream.	6.9
4.1	Pass through an old field, now overgrown with red cedars.	6.7
4.2	Cross a swampy area on puncheon, and cross a stream on rocks.	6.6
4.4	Cross a dirt road (leads to youth camp).	6.4
4.7	Cross a swampy area on puncheon.	6.1

SECTION HIGHLIGHTS

Pochuck Mountain Shelter →

Built in 1988-89 by local volunteers with assistance from the ATC Mid-Atlantic Trail Crew; accommodates 6; no water source at the shelter. The nearest water is a spigot at a house, 0.5 mile to the south at the foot of the mountain, on Lake Wallkill Road (Liberty Corners Road). Next shelter: north, 11.8 miles (Wawayanda Shelter); south, 13.2 miles (High Point Shelter).

Lake Wallkill Road (Liberty Corners Road) →

A water pump that used to be here was removed because of water pollution. Water is available from a spigot at a house (owned by the state of New Jersey) a short distance to the east (compass-north), up a steep driveway.

Liberty Loop Trail →

A 2.5-mile loop around the Wallkill River National Wildlife Refuge, part of it following the former right-of-way of the Lehigh and New England Railroad. The Lehigh & New England received its name in 1905 after Lehigh Coal & Navigation bought its predecessor, the Pennsylvania, Poughkeepsie & Boston (known as the "Pickles, Pork & Beans" line), which had served the "drowned lands" in the mid-nineteenth century, linking Lehigh Gap, Pennsylvania, with the New Haven Railroad. The line was abandoned in 1961.

Wallkill River National Wildlife Refuge →

The only federal wildlife refuge on the entire Appalachian Trail. The A.T. squares around part of the refuge that was once a sod farm, the piping and irrigation canals of which are still apparent. A dazzling variety of birds lives in the wetlands here (see next page). Be aware that hunting is permitted in the fall, and bugs are fierce during summer months. Pets are not allowed, except for those accompanying long-distance hikers on the Appalachian Trail (those must be leashed). Jogging, bicycling, horseback riding, camping, overnight parking, and the use of motor vehicles are prohibited. Refuge headquarters are in Sussex, N.J. (see mile 3.8 above).

N-S

TRAIL DESCRIPTION

5.0	Reach the summit of **Pochuck Mountain** (elev. 1,194 ft.). A side trail leads west 40 feet to a viewpoint over the west ridge of the mountain.	**5.8**
5.2	Cross a dirt road and puncheon in a swampy area—one of the few potential water sources on the mountain.	**5.6**
5.5	Pass a stone foundation to the west of the Trail.	**5.3**
5.7	Reach an overlook at the crest of a rise, with western views across the Wallkill Valley to High Point and the Kittatinny and Shawangunk mountains.	**5.1**
6.0	Cross a woods road.	**4.8**
6.3	Reach the summit of the western ridge of **Pochuck Mountain** and begin to descend.	**4.5**
6.5	A blue-blazed side trail on the west side of the A.T. leads 0.1 mile to the **Pochuck Mountain Shelter**.	**4.3**
6.9	Cross an open field on the hillside.	**3.9**
7.0	The A.T. intersects with paved **Lake Wallkill Road** (also known as Liberty Corners Road) at the foot of a steep slope. Turn right and follow road for 120 feet, then turn left and reenter woods.	**3.8**
7.1	Reach the northern edge of a swampy area (elev. 400 ft.). Southbound hikers cross the swamp on puncheon. Northbound hikers leave the swamp and reenter woods.	**3.7**
7.5	The A.T. intersects with the **Liberty Loop Trail**, a dirt road. Southbound hikers turn left onto the dirt road, entering the **Wallkill River National Wildlife Refuge**. Northbound hikers turn right, leaving the dirt road, and follow puncheon (bog bridges) for about 0.4 mile over a swampy area.	**3.3**

S-N

The amazing variety of birds at the Wallkill Flats can be seen in this list of species observed there by the U.S. Fish and Wildlife Service. Those marked with an asterisk (*) are frequently seen:

Grebes—Pied-Billed Grebe

Bitterns, Herons, and Egrets—*American Bittern, *Least Bittern, *Great Blue Heron, Great Egret, Snowy Egret, Cattle Egret, *Green Heron, Black-Crowned Night-Heron

Ibises and Spoonbills—Glossy Ibis

New World Vultures—Black Vulture, *Turkey Vulture

Swans, Geese, and Ducks—Snow Goose, *Canada Goose, Brant, *Mute Swan, *Wood Duck, Gadwall, American Wigeon, *American Black Duck,*Mallard, Blue-Winged Teal, Northern Shoveler, Northern Pintail, Green-Winged Teal, Ring-Necked Duck, Bufflehead, Common Goldeneye, *Hooded Merganser, *Common Merganser, Ruddy Duck

Osprey, Kites, Hawks, and Eagles—Osprey, Bald Eagle, Northern Harrier, Sharp-Shinned Hawk, *Cooper's Hawk, Northern Goshawk, Red-Shouldered Hawk, *Broad-Winged Hawk, *Red-Tailed Hawk, Rough-Legged Hawk, Golden Eagle

Falcons and Caracaras—*American Kestrel, Merlin, Peregrine Falcon

Gallinaceous Birds—*Ring-Necked Pheasant, *Ruffed Grouse, *Wild Turkey, Northern Bobwhite

Rails—*King Rail, *Virginia Rail, *Sora, *Common Moorhen, American Coot

Plovers—Black-Bellied Plover, American Golden-Plover, Semipalmated Plover, *Killdeer

Sandpipers and Phalaropes—Greater Yellowlegs, Lesser Yellowlegs, Solitary Sandpiper, *Spotted Sandpiper, *Upland Sandpiper, Hudsonian Godwit, Semipalmated Sandpiper, Least Sandpiper, Baird's Sandpiper, Pectoral Sandpiper, Buff-Breasted Sandpiper, Common Snipe, *American Woodcock

Skuas, Jaegers, Gulls, and Terns—Ring-Billed Gull, Herring Gull, Great Black-Backed Gull

Pigeons and Doves—*Rock Dove, *Mourning Dove

Cuckoos and Anis—*Black-Billed Cuckoo, *Yellow-Billed Cuckoo

Barn Owls—Barn Owl

Typical Owls—*Eastern Screech-Owl, *Great Horned Owl, Snowy Owl, *Barred Owl, Long-Eared Owl, Short-Eared Owl, Northern Saw-Whet Owl

Nightjars—*Common Nighthawk, Whip-Poor-Will

Swifts—*Chimney Swift

Hummingbirds—*Ruby-Throated Hummingbird

Kingfishers—*Belted Kingfisher

Woodpeckers—Red-Headed Woodpecker, *Red-Bellied Woodpecker, Yellow-Bellied Sapsucker, *Downy Woodpecker, *Hairy Woodpecker, *Northern Flicker, *Pileated Woodpecker

Tyrant Flycatchers—Olive-Sided Flycatcher, *Eastern Wood-Pewee, Yellow-Bellied Flycatcher, Acadian Flycatcher, *Alder Flycatcher, *Willow Flycatcher,

*Least Flycatcher, *Eastern Phoebe, *Great Crested Flycatcher, Western Kingbird, *Eastern Kingbird

Shrikes—Northern Shrike

Vireos—*White-Eyed Vireo, *Yellow-Throated Vireo, Blue-Headed Vireo, *Warbling Vireo, Philadelphia Vireo, *Red-Eyed Vireo

Crows, Jays, and Magpies—*Blue Jay, *American Crow, Fish Crow

Larks—Horned Lark

Swallows—*Purple Martin, *Tree Swallow, *Northern Rough-Winged Swallow, *Bank Swallow, *Cliff Swallow, *Barn Swallow

Titmice and Chickadees—*Black-Capped Chickadee, *Tufted Titmouse

Nuthatches—Red-Breasted Nuthatch, *White-Breasted Nuthatch

Creepers—*Brown Creeper

Wrens—*Carolina Wren, *House Wren, Winter Wren, *Sedge Wren, *Marsh Wren

Kinglets—Golden-Crowned Kinglet, Ruby- Crowned Kinglet

Old World Warblers—*Blue-Gray Gnatcatcher

Thrushes—*Eastern Bluebird, *Veery, Gray-Cheeked Thrush, Swainson's Thrush, Hermit Thrush, *Wood Thrush, *American Robin

Mimic Thrushes—*Gray Catbird, *Northern Mockingbird, *Brown Thrasher

Starlings—*European Starling

Wagtails and Pipits—American Pipit

Waxwings—*Cedar Waxwing

Wood Warblers—*Blue-Winged Warbler, *Golden-Winged Warbler, Tennessee Warbler, Nashville Warbler, Northern Parula, *Yellow Warbler, *Chestnut- Sided Warbler, Magnolia Warbler, Cape May Warbler, Black-Throated Blue Warbler, Yellow-Rumped Warbler, Black-Throated Green Warbler, Blackburnian Warbler, Pine Warbler, *Prairie Warbler, Palm Warbler, Bay-Breasted Warbler, Blackpoll Warbler, *Cerulean Warbler, *Black and-White Warbler, *American Redstart, *Prothonotary Warbler, *Worm-Eating Warbler, *Ovenbird, *Northern Waterthrush, *Louisiana Waterthrush, *Kentucky Warbler, Mourning Warbler, *Common Yellowthroat, *Hooded Warbler, Wilson's Warbler, *Canada Warbler, *Yellow-Breasted Chat

Tanagers—*Scarlet Tanager

Sparrows and Towhees—*Eastern Towhee, American Tree Sparrow, *Chipping Sparrow, *Field Sparrow, Vesper Sparrow, *Savannah Sparrow, *Grasshopper Sparrow, Henslow's Sparrow, Fox Sparrow, *Song Sparrow, Lincoln's Sparrow, *Swamp Sparrow, White-Throated Sparrow, White-Crowned Sparrow, Dark-Eyed Junco, Lapland Longspur, Snow Bunting

Grosbeaks and Allies—*Northern Cardinal, *Rose-Breasted Grosbeak, *Blue Grosbeak, *Indigo Bunting, Dickcissel

Blackbirds and Orioles—Bobolink, *Red-Winged Blackbird, *Eastern Meadowlark, Rusty Blackbird, *Common Grackle, *Brown-Headed Cowbird, *Orchard Oriole, *Baltimore Oriole

Finches—*Purple Finch, *House Finch, Red Crossbill, Common Redpoll, Pine Siskin, *American Goldfinch, Evening Grosbeak

Old World Sparrows—*House Sparrow

Wallkill River →

The main waterway of the Wallkill Valley and the "drowned lands." Here, as in the Cumberland Valley of Pennsylvania and the Valley of Virginia near Roanoke, the A.T. is crossing the Great Valley of the Appalachians, a major geological feature that comprises a number of connected valleys between New York and Alabama. The action of glaciers is apparent in the geology here, particularly in the mucky soils of the Vernon Valley, a former glacial lake. Pochuck Mountain, a block of resistant metamorphic gneiss, represents the high point and drainage divide between Vernon Valley and Kittatinny Valley.

Oil City Road →

Leads west 2.0 miles to Unionville, New York. A nearby pumping station for the Olean–Bayonne oil pipeline of the Standard Oil Company in the 1880s gave "Oil City" its name. A massive "tank farm" once stood nearby. Remains of the pumping station, on property of Carnegie Industries, can still be seen near the A.T. (mile 9.5).

Southern end of section →

The Trail crosses N.J. 284, 0.9 mile south of the center of Unionville, New York. Parking for four or five cars is available in a dirt turnout just north of the Trail crossing (overnight parking is not encouraged). Groceries, meals, and a post office (ZIP Code 10988) are available in Unionville. No accommodations are available at the southern end of the section. No public transportation is available.

N-S	TRAIL DESCRIPTION	
7.8	The Trail makes a 90-degree turn.	**3.0**
8.3	The Trail makes a 90-degree turn.	**2.5**
9.0	The A.T. intersects with paved **Oil City Road**. Southbound hikers cross the New York state line before reaching the road, then turn left and follow the paved road. Northbound hikers turn right from the road onto **Liberty Loop Trail** (a dirt road), cross the New Jersey state line, and enter **Wallkill River National Wildlife Refuge.**	**1.8**
9.3	Cross bridge over the **Wallkill River** on Oil City Road.	**1.5**
9.5	The A.T. intersects with a private road leading into the property of Carnegie Industries. Southbound hikers turn left onto the private road and cross the New Jersey state line. Northbound hikers cross New York state line, then turn right onto **Oil City Road**.	**1.3**
9.7	The A.T. intersects with a private road just north of a bridge over a small stream. Southbound hikers turn right, leaving the road, and reenter the woods on a footpath. Northbound hikers turn left onto the private road.	**1.1**
10.1	Cross a field.	**0.7**
10.2	Reach the top of a hill, and begin to descend.	**0.6**
10.3	Cross paved Oil City Road (different than the road at mile 9.0–9.5 with the same name).	**0.5**
10.8	Reach N.J. 284, the **southern end of section**, just south of a bridge over a brook. Southbound hikers cross the road and follow the Trail uphill into woods (New Jersey Section Three below). Northbound hikers cross a bridge over a brook and follow puncheon through swampy thickets.	**0.0**

N.J. 284 (Unionville, New York) to N.J. 23 (High Point, New Jersey)

9.8 MILES

This section of the Trail crosses wetlands, farm country, and low hills. It parallels the New York–New Jersey state line. At the southern end, it traverses the eastern face of the Kittatinny Ridge and passes just below High Point Monument, which marks the highest elevation in New Jersey (1,803 feet). The walking here is mostly pleasant and easy.

This section was the first portion of the A.T. in New Jersey to be relocated within the protected Appalachian Trail corridor acquired by the state of New Jersey. It was opened on October 2, 1982, in a ceremony attended by the governor, at which time a cooperative agreement between the NY–NJ TC and the state for the maintenance of the Trail was signed.

Road Approaches—Both the northern and southern ends of this section are accessible by vehicle. The Trail in this section also crosses numerous secondary roads and lanes, but parking along those roads is not recommended.

Maps—For route navigation, refer to Maps 4 and 5 with this guide. For area detail, refer to the following USGS 7½-minute topographic quadrangles: Unionville, New York–New Jersey; Port Jervis South, New Jersey–New York–Pennsylvania.

Shelters and Campsites—This section has one shelter, High Point Shelter, at mile 8.1 below. No camping is permitted elsewhere in the section. No fires are permitted.

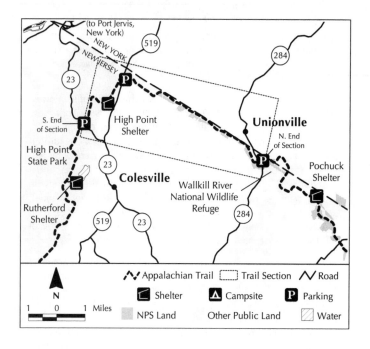

Appalachian Trail Trail Section Road
Shelter Campsite Parking
NPS Land Other Public Land Water

N

1 0 1 Miles

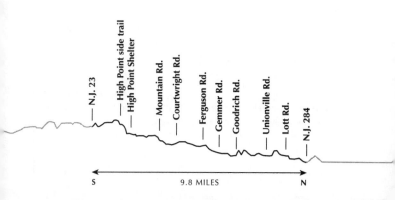

S 9.8 MILES N

SECTION HIGHLIGHTS

Note—*Because of the orientation of the Trail in this section, the "northern" end of the section is actually farther south than the "southern" end. See page 14 for an explanation of how compass directions are used in this guide.*

Northern end of section →

The Trail crosses N.J. 284, 0.4 mile south of the New York–New Jersey boundary and 0.9 mile south of the center of Unionville, New York. Parking for four or five cars is available in a dirt turnout just north of the Trail crossing (overnight parking is not encouraged). Public transportation is not available. Groceries, sandwiches, and a post office (ZIP Code 10988) are available in Unionville. Unionville also may be reached via Lott Road (also known as Jersey Avenue), at mile 1.0 below. A deli, with a limited selection of groceries, is on N.Y. 284 at the New York–New Jersey boundary, 0.4 mile west of the Trail crossing. No accommodations are available.

Railroad grade →

This rail line was built by the New Jersey Midland Railroad about 1872. It was originally intended to serve as part of a through-route from Jersey City to Oswego, New York. However, through traffic to Oswego was soon routed *via* Cornwall, New York, and the line became the Hanford Branch of the New York, Susquehanna and Western Railway, providing primarily local service. It was abandoned in 1958.

Lott Road →

Leads west 0.4 mile to Unionville, New York. Follow Lott Road to west (compass-north) for 0.3 mile, then turn left along N.Y. 284 for 0.1 mile.

Old quarry roads →

This area was famous in the nineteenth century for its production of bluestone, widely used as a paving material.

N-S

TRAIL DESCRIPTION

0.0 The **northern end of section** is at N.J. 284. Southbound hikers enter woods and ascend to an overgrown field. Northbound hikers cross a bridge over a brook and follow puncheon through swampy thickets (New Jersey Section Two above). **9.8**

0.3 The Trail intersects with an abandoned **railroad grade**. Southbound hikers bear right and follow the railroad grade. Northbound hikers bear left, leaving the railroad grade, and descend toward an open field. **9.5**

0.8 The Trail intersects with an abandoned **railroad grade**. Southbound hikers bear left, leaving the railroad grade, follow a stone wall parallel to the railroad grade for 350 feet, then turn left into the woods. Northbound hikers follow the railroad grade. **9.0**

1.0 The Trail turns right onto paved **Lott Road** (also known as Jersey Avenue). It follows the road for 150 feet, crossing a bridge over a stream, then turns right, and reenters the woods. **8.8**

1.1 Cross an open field. **8.7**

1.2 Cross several **old quarry roads**. **8.6**

1.5 Reach the crest of a hill, and begin to descend. **8.3**

1.7 Cross paved Quarry Road. **8.1**

1.8 Pass an old quarry pit below, to the west of the Trail. **8.0**

1.9 Cross paved **Unionville Road** (County 651) diagonally to the left. **7.9**

2.1 The Trail reaches a hilltop above overgrown fields and an abandoned apple orchard. **7.7**

2.4 Cross dirt Goldsmith Lane. **7.4**

S-N

Vernie Swamp

Unionville Road →
Leads west (compass-north) 0.7 mile to Unionville, New York.

Vernie Swamp →
The A.T. follows more than 112 bog bridges (or puncheon) through this wetland. In the past, beaver activity has been a problem, causing flooding of the bridges, but recent reconstruction projects by Trail maintainers have elevated the puncheon to compensate.

Wolf Pit Hill →
Gets its name from a time when a bounty on wolves was collected during the early nineteenth century. The hill provides an excellent view of High Point Monument to the south (compass-west) and Pochuck Mountain to the north (compass-east).

N-S	TRAIL DESCRIPTION	
2.5	Reach northern end of **Vernie Swamp**. Southbound hikers follow puncheon across the swamp for next 0.2 mile. Northbound hikers ascend gradually through an overgrown field.	7.3
2.7	Cross gravel Goldsmith Road at the southern end of **Vernie Swamp**. Southbound hikers climb along right side of a field, keeping trees and low stone wall (New York–New Jersey boundary) to the right. Northbound hikers cross a bridge over a stream and follow puncheon across Vernie Swamp.	7.1
2.9	Reach the crest of **Wolf Pit Hill** in an open field.	6.9
3.0	Cross a concrete dam (outlet of pond).	6.8
3.2	Cross paved Goodrich Road.	6.6
3.5	Cross three wooden bridges over streams.	6.3
3.8	Reach the crest of a rise, and begin to descend.	6.0
3.9	Cross a stream on a wooden bridge.	5.9
4.0	Pass an intersection of stone walls.	5.8
4.1	Cross a wooden bridge over a brook north of an overgrown field.	5.7
4.2	The Trail turns right and follows paved Gemmer Road for 200 feet. Southbound hikers turn left and reenter the woods, passing through a swampy area. Northbound hikers turn left and follow posts across an overgrown field.	5.6
4.3	Cross a small brook.	5.5
4.4	Cross a stone wall marking the boundary of an overgrown field.	5.4

SECTION HIGHLIGHTS

Cultivated field →

This section of Trail corridor is being farmed under lease with the former owner, whose family has worked the land for five generations. The Trail follows mostly state-owned land through this corridor, although the corridor includes small pockets of federal property as well. The New York–New Jersey Trail Conference and other groups have suggested that lands along the state line corridor be consolidated into a new state park, which they propose to call the Great Valley of the Appalachians State Park.

Low hills →

The low hills of this section of the Trail between the Wallkill Valley and Kittatinny Mountain are underlain by rocks of grey shale, which is apparent in outcroppings and in chips along the way.

Farmland along the Appalachian Trail offers hikers an interesting change of pace from more typical ridgetop traverses and woodland walks. Cropland and pasture open up far-reaching pastoral views. Other agricultural properties, such as New England sugarbushes—woodlands where farmers tap trees to retrieve maple sap—give intriguing hints of America's agrarian past. All of those agricultural lands contribute to the cultural richness of the Appalachian Trail experience.

The Appalachian Trail Conference supports agriculture on long-established farms and settings desirable for hiking. When guided by government agencies, agriculture on trail corridor lands plays a helpful role in maintaining the views and features hikers come to see. It also furthers good community relations, dovetailing recreational and community needs while adding little burden on volunteer time and energy.

—From *Appalachian Trail Design, Construction, and Maintenance,* by Robert Proudman and William Birchard.

N-S

TRAIL DESCRIPTION

4.8 Turn right onto Ferguson Road for 120 feet. Southbound hikers turn left, cross a stile, and follow blazes across a pasture. Northbound hikers turn left and reenter woods, soon beginning to descend.　　**5.0**

4.9 Cross puncheon and a bridge over a stream.　　**4.9**

5.0 Reach an intersection of stone walls. Southbound hikers bear right and skirt a **cultivated field**. Northbound hikers bear left for about 200 feet, then bear right across a pasture.　　**4.8**

5.1 Cross an overgrown stone wall. Southbound hikers skirt the upper field, following the treeline on the left. Northbound hikers enter the lower field and skirt the field by keeping the treeline to the right.　　**4.7**

5.3 Pass a pond to the west, between fields. Southbound hikers emerge onto another field and turn right, skirting the field. In another 300 feet, they turn right, and cross a stile over a barbed-wire fence, then turn left, and ascend along the left side of a pasture. Northbound hikers bear right and skirt the edge of a field, then bear left and continue along the right side of the field.　　**4.5**

5.5 Cross a stile over a barbed-wire fence near the crest of a pasture, above fields.　　**4.3**

5.6 Cross a stone wall at the edge of the woods.　　**4.2**

5.8 Follow blazes carefully across and along many old stone walls in an area of **low hills**.　　**4.0**

S-N

SECTION HIGHLIGHTS

County 519 →

Parking for day hikes is available at the Trail crossing here. Overnight parking is discouraged.

Stone walls →

You may see signs near here of pastures from a failed attempt to raise elk and reindeer by the family that donated the land for High Point State Park in 1923.

High Point Shelter →

Built in 1936 by the Civilian Conservation Corps; a stone shelter with a wooden floor; accommodates 8; water is available from streams near the shelter. Next shelter: north, 12.3 miles (Pochuck Mountain Shelter); south, 4.3 miles (Rutherford Shelter).

Monument Trail →

A 3.5-mile loop converging at the A.T. The branch to the north leads to High Point Monument, the highest elevation in New Jersey (elev. 1,803 ft.). The branch to the south leads to Lake Marcia.

Observation platform →

Excellent 360-degree view. Kittatinny Valley lies to compass-east, with Pochuck Mountain in the distance and Wawayanda Mountain on the horizon. The New York City skyline may be visible to the southeast. To the southwest is the Delaware Water Gap. In the foreground to compass-west is Lake Marcia, with the Pocono Mountains of Pennsylvania in the distance. The Catskill Plateau lies to the northwest. High Point Monument dominates the ridge to compass-north.

High Point Monument →

Completed in 1930, High Point Monument was built through the generosity of Col. Anthony R. Kuser and his wife, Susie Dryden Kuser, and is dedicated to "New Jersey's heroes by land, sea, and air in all wars in our country." Col. and Mrs. Kuser also donated the original 10,500 acres of High Point State Park to the people of New Jersey in 1923. The red-and-green-blazed Monument Trail leads to the monu-

N-S	TRAIL DESCRIPTION	
6.0	Cross dirt-and-gravel Courtwright Road.	**3.8**
6.1	Cross two streams to the north of an overgrown field.	**3.7**
6.3	Cross several stone walls.	**3.5**
6.7	Pass through fields, skirting trees on a rise.	**3.1**
6.8	Cross paved **County 519,** below Kittatinny Mountain, diagonally to the left. Southbound hikers enter the woods, ascending on switchbacks. Northbound hikers enter fields.	**3.0**
7.0	Skirt fields near a swampy area.	**2.8**
7.3	Pass through gaps in several **stone walls** at crest of ridge.	**2.5**
7.8	Cross an intermittent brook at the head of a ravine, north of a stone wall.	**2.0**
8.0	Turn at a large pile of rocks at the foot of a slope.	**1.8**
8.1	A blue-blazed side trail leads east 0.1 mile to **High Point Shelter**.	**1.7**
8.6	The Trail intersects with the red-and-green-blazed **Monument Trail**.	**1.2**
8.8	Reach a wooden **observation platform** on the ridge near **High Point Monument**.	**1.0**

ment, but much the same panorama of New Jersey, Pennsylvania, and New York is provided from a wooden observation platform directly on the A.T. During the summer season, refreshments are available at a concession stand near the monument.

Southern end of section →

The Trail crosses N.J. 23 at the southern driveway of High Point State Park headquarters. Water is available there. Please sign the Trail register at the office. A parking lot specifically for A.T. hikers is located just south of park headquarters (registration required for overnight parking). Supermarkets and a coin laundry are located along N.J. 23, 4.3 miles northwest of the Trail crossing. Groceries are also available in Colesville, 2.5 miles southeast of the Trail crossing on N.J. 23. Supermarkets, restaurants, and a post office (ZIP Code 12771) are located in Port Jervis, New York, about seven miles northwest of the Trail crossing (follow N.J. 23 north to junction with U.S. 6; continue west on U.S. 6). The park headquarters will accept and hold packages for hikers if marked "hold for arrival" with the name of the hiker and the approximate date of arrival specified (address: High Point State Park, Sussex, NJ 07461). Bus service to New York City, operated by Short Line Bus System, (201) 444-7005, is available at Port Jervis. Rail service to New York City (*via* Hoboken), operated by the Metro-North Railroad, (212) 532-4900 or (800) 638-7646, is also available. Motels are located on N.J. 23, 1.4 miles south and 4.4 miles north of the Trail crossing.

N-S

TRAIL DESCRIPTION

9.8 The **southern end of section** is at paved N.J. 23. South-bound hikers cross the road, continue across the lawn to the left of the driveway, and reenter the woods (see New Jersey Section Four). Northbound hikers bear northeast across the lawn for 250 feet and enter the woods.

0.0

S-N

N.J. 23 (High Point)
to U.S. 206 (Culvers Gap)

14.3 MILES

The Trail runs along the Kittatinny Ridge through High Point State Park and Stokes State Forest. It follows a rocky route through hickory and scrub-oak forests, with some hemlocks and pitch pines. There are many good viewpoints on both sides of the ridge. The highest point in this section is 1,653 feet at Sunrise Mountain.

Many side trails intersect the A.T. in this section, connecting to woods roads, lakes, and other popular sites in the state parklands. Descriptions of those trails may be found in brochures available at the headquarters of High Point State Park and Stokes State Forest.

Road Approaches—In addition to the northern and southern ends of the section, road access is also available at Deckertown Turnpike, at mile 5.3, and Sunrise Mountain Road, at mile 13.9.

Maps—For route navigation, refer to Map 5 with this guide. For area detail, refer to the following USGS 7½-minute topographic quadrangles: Port Jervis South, New Jersey–New York–Pennsylvania; Branchville, New Jersey; Culvers Gap, New Jersey–Pennsylvania. Other references are NY–NJ TC Trail Maps 17 and 18 (Kittatinny Trails—North).

Shelters and Campsites—This section has three shelters: Rutherford Shelter (mile 2.6 below), Mashipacong Shelter (mile 5.5 below), and Gren Anderson Shelter (mile 11.3 below). No camping is permitted in the section, except at shelters and at the Sawmill Camping Area (fee charged), 0.4 mile off the A.T. at mile 0.9 below.

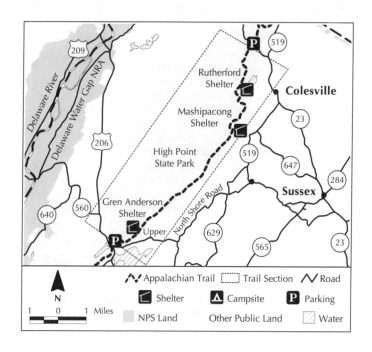

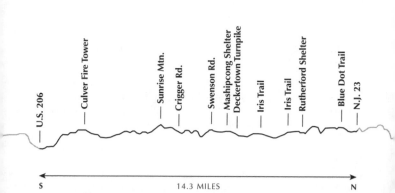

SECTION HIGHLIGHTS

Northern end of section →
A separate parking area for A.T. hikers, connected to the A.T. by a short side trail, is located off the south side of N.J. 23, just south of park headquarters (registration required for overnight parking). Bus service to New York City, operated by Short Line Bus System, (201) 444-7005, is available at Port Jervis, New York, about seven miles northwest of the Trail crossing of N.J. 23 (follow N.J. 23 north to junction with U.S. 6; continue west on U.S. 6). Rail service from Port Jervis to New York City is operated by the Metro-North Railroad, (212) 532-4900 or (800) 638-7646. Supermarkets and a coin laundry are on N.J. 23, 4.3 miles northwest of the Trail crossing. Groceries are also available in Colesville, 2.5 miles southeast of the Trail crossing on N.J. 23. Supermarkets, restaurants, and a post office (ZIP Code 12771) are located in Port Jervis. Motels are located on N.J. 23, 1.4 miles south and 4.4 miles north of the Trail crossing.

High Point State Park →
See mile 6.0 below. Park headquarters will accept and hold resupply packages for hikers if marked "hold for arrival," with the name of the hiker and the approximate date of arrival specified (address: High Point State Park, Sussex, NJ 07461).

Mashipacong Trail →
Leads 1.5 miles west along an old farm road to Sawmill Road.

Iris Trail →
Parallels A.T for 4.0 miles south of park headquarters, below the ridgeline, crossing the A.T. at mile 3.4 and 4.6; it can be used to make a loop hike.

Blue Dot Trail →
Descends steeply for 0.4 mile to Sawmill Camping Area, near Sawmill Lake; swimming, restrooms, purified water, tent camping available (fee charged). Reservations have priority.

| TRAIL DESCRIPTION |

High Point State Park

0.0 The **northern end of section** (elev. 1,500 ft.) is at the **14.3**
intersection of the A.T. with N.J. 23. Southbound hikers
proceed south across a lawn of **High Point State Park**
headquarters, soon entering woods. Northbound hikers
proceed north across a lawn and soon enter woods (New
Jersey Section Three, above).

0.1 Reach Trail intersection, marked by a four-foot-high **14.2**
white pipe to the east of the Trail. The yellow-blazed
Mashipacong Trail intersects on the west side of the A.T.
The red-on-white blazed **Iris Trail** intersects on the east
side of the A.T., (see mile 2.6 below).

0.6 Reach northern end of ridge (elev. 1,610 ft.). Southbound **13.7**
hikers continue south along the ridge. Northbound hikers
turn east, leaving the ridge, and descend.

0.9 **Blue Dot Trail** intersects on the west side of the A.T. **13.4**

Sawmill Lake →

Popular recreation area in High Point State Park. Site of an old cedar swamp, impounded by the Civilian Conservation Corps in the 1930s.

Pocono Mountains →

Pennsylvania's Poconos range in height from 1,900 to 2,200 feet above sea level. Like the New Jersey highlands and "skylands," glacial action during the last Ice Age marked them dramatically, and their scenery makes them a popular vacation area.

Rutherford Shelter →

Reached from the west *via* blue-blazed trail (leading steeply down from Dutch Shoe Rock). Built in 1967 by the state of New Jersey; a log shelter with a wooden floor; 0.4 mile from A.T. on blue-blazed side trail; accommodates 6; water from nearby spring. Next shelter: north, 4.3 miles (High Point Shelter); south, 2.9 miles (Mashipacong Shelter).

Iris Trail →

See mile 0.1 above. From the intersection, it leads 0.7 mile north to Lake Rutherford; to the south, it follows an old woods road, crossing the A.T. again at mile 4.6.

Deckertown Turnpike →

A parking area is on the north side of the road crossing. A water pump that was here for many years has been removed.

N-S

| | TRAIL DESCRIPTION | |

1.0 Reach a viewpoint to the west over **Sawmill Lake**.   **13.3**

1.3 Cross a low point (elev.1,470 ft.) between ridges.   **13.0**

1.4 Reach a west-facing viewpoint (elev. 1,622 ft.) over an   **12.9**
interior valley, with the **Pocono Mountains** visible in the
distance to the southwest. Southbound hikers proceed
south along the eastern ridge. Northbound hikers begin
a steep descent into the interior valley.

2.4 Reach a viewpoint from open rocks on the east side of   **11.9**
the Trail. To the northeast, Lake Rutherford, water supply
for the town of Sussex, is visible.

2.6 Reach Dutch Shoe Rock, with views to the northeast of   **11.7**
High Point and the Wallkill Valley. A blue-blazed side trail
on the east side of the A.T. descends 0.4 mile to **Rutherford
Shelter** and a nearby spring.

3.4 Turn right onto an old woods road, also follwed by the   **10.9**
red-on-white-blazed **Iris Trail** (elev. 1,430 ft.) . In 300 feet,
turn left onto footpath.

3.8 At a low point the low point (elev. 1,290 ft.), cross a   **10.5**
stream on logs.

4.2 On the ridgeline (elev. 1,400 ft.), cross a cleared strip of   **10.1**
land, the route of a buried pipeline. A short trail to the east
leads to an east-facing viewpoint over a farm landscape
in the Wallkill Valley.

4.5 Please sign the Trail register on a tree on the west side   **9.8**
of the Trail.

4.6 The A.T. intersects with the red-on-white-blazed **Iris   **9.7**
Trail**.

5.3 Cross the paved **Deckertown Turnpike** diagonally to the   **8.9**
left.

S-N

Mashipacong Shelter →

Built in 1936; stone shelter with wooden floor; accommodates 8; no water. Next shelter: north, 2.9 miles (Rutherford Shelter); south, 5.8 miles (Gren Anderson Shelter).

High Point State Park →

Comprises 14,218 acres of woodland atop Kittatinny Mountain. It was the first state park in New Jersey (dedicated in 1923). Among its scenic highlights are the highest-elevation cedar swamp of its kind in the world, glacial Lake Marcia, and High Point Monument, at the state's highest point, built in 1930 and dedicated to New Jersey's wartime veterans. Fishing, boating, skating, picnicking, hiking, cross-country skiing, and hunting are seasonal activities.

Stokes State Forest →

Covering 15,482 acres along Kittatinny Mountain, the state forest was purchased in 1907 and named after Gov. Edward C. Stokes. Old-growth forest along the ridge was cut for timber by the mid-nineteenth century, but the poor soil there made the area mostly unsuitable for farming. The park office is about 0.5 mile west of the southern end of the section, just north of U.S. 206.

Sunrise Mountain →

The highest point of the section provides a panoramic view, including the New Jersey Highlands and Wallkill Valley to the east and the Delaware River and Pocono Mountains to the west. Restrooms are located at a parking area 0.1 mile north, which connects to the A.T. by way of a path at mile 8.8. A 1930s Civilian Conservation Corps (CCC) shelter is at the summit. It has a roof but no walls and provides protection from rain, except in high winds. Camping is prohibited.

Tinsley Trail →

Descends to west, crossing Sunrise Mountain Road in 60 yards and continuing to Skellinger Road, about 0.5 mile from Lake Ocquittunk (site for trailer-camping and rental cabins in Stokes State Forest).

N-S	TRAIL DESCRIPTION	
5.5	Reach **Mashipacong Shelter**.	8.8
6.0	Reach southern boundary of **High Point State Park** (northern boundary of **Stokes State Forest**).	8.3
6.2	The A.T. route coincides with a woods road (Swenson Road) for 225 feet.	8.1
6.8	The Trail skirts the east side of a rise (elev. 1,548 ft.).	7.5
7.2	Cross the outlet of a swamp on the east side of the Trail at a low point (elev. 1,350 ft.) between rises.	7.1
7.4	Reach top of a rise and cross several stone walls.	6.9
8.1	Cross dirt Crigger Road, below Sunrise Mountain.	6.2
8.8	A path to a parking area intersects on the west side of the Trail.	5.5
8.9	Reach a day-use shelter at the summit of **Sunrise Mountain** (elev. 1,653 ft.). Southbound hikers continue on the Trail from the southeast corner of the shelter, descending over rocks. Northbound hikers continue on a wide footpath from the northeast corner of the shelter.	5.4
9.9	The A.T intersects with the yellow-blazed **Tinsley Trail**.	4.4

Sunrise Mountain

S-N

Stony Brook Trail →

Leads west 0.3 mile to Sunrise Mountain Road and continues 1.0 mile to Stony Lake, a popular day-use area with swimming, fishing, and a bathhouse; for 200 feet, it coincides with the blue-blazed trail to the shelter.

Gren Anderson Shelter →

Built in 1958 by the New York Section of the Green Mountain Club, of which Anderson was a member; log shelter, 650 feet from A.T. on blue-blazed side trail; accommodates 8; water from spring on side trail 200 feet beyond shelter. Next shelter: north, 5.8 miles (Mashipacong Shelter); south, 6.7 miles (Brink Road Shelter).

Tower Trail →

Descends to the west, crosses Sunrise Mountain Road, and intersects with Stony Brook Trail east of Stony Lake.

Culver Fire Tower →

Erected by the Civilian Conservation Corps in 1934. Lake Owassa is visible to the southwest, just left of Kittatinny Ridge, and Lake Kittatinny is visible to the right of the ridge.

Southern end of section →

A parking area is adjacent to the A.T., 0.3 mile north of the Trail crossing of U.S. 206, on Sunrise Mountain Road, just north of its intersection with County 636 (Upper North Shore Road). Registration at Stokes State Forest office is required for overnight parking; the office is 0.5 mile west on U.S. 206. A limited selection of groceries may be obtained at Worthington's Bakery, immediately west of the crossing. A grocery store is located on U.S. 206, 1.6 miles southeast of the crossing. Meals are available at a restaurant 0.1 mile west of the crossing. A hunting store, which sells freeze-dried foods and some camping equipment, is 0.2 mile west. Branchville has a post office (ZIP Code 07826) and a coin laundry, 3.4 miles southeast of the Trail crossing of U.S. 206. Motels are located on U.S. 206, 2.5 miles east and 1.9 miles west of the Trail crossing.

N-S

	TRAIL DESCRIPTION	
10.0	The Trail passes a viewpoint to the west.	4.3
11.3	The brown-blazed **Stony Brook Trail** and the blue-blazed side trail to the **Gren Anderson Shelter** and an adjacent spring intersect on the west side of the A.T.	3.0
11.4	Cross Stony Brook.	2.9
12.3	The green-blazed **Tower Trail** intersects on the west side of the A.T. at a viewpoint to the west in pines. Please sign the Trail register on a tree on the west side of the A.T.	2.0
12.4	Emerge onto a clearing, and reach the **Culver Fire Tower**, with excellent views.	1.9
12.5	Unmarked trail, which intersects on west side of A.T., leads 75 feet to an excellent viewpoint.	1.8
13.4	Reach viewpoint to west over Kittatinny Lake, a residential area.	0.9
13.9	Reach paved Sunrise Mountain Road. Leads to parking atop Sunrise Mountain (mile 8.9 above), and on U.S. 206 (mile 14.3 below). Turn left, and follow road for 125 feet, then turn right, and reenter woods.	0.4
14.1	An unmarked trail to a parking area intersects on the east side of the A.T.	0.2
14.3	**Southern end of section**. Reach intersection of County 636 (Upper North Shore Road) with U.S. 206. Southbound hikers proceed east on U.S. 206 for a short distance, then turn right and ascend (New Jersey Section Five below). Northbound hikers proceed north on footpath from the northwest corner of the intersection.	0.0

S-N

U.S. 206 (Culvers Gap) to Millbrook-Blairstown Road

14.5 MILES

The route follows the wooded ridge of Kittatinny Mountain, passing through oak and hickory hardwood forests, with some conifers, such as pitch pine, white pine, red cedar, and hemlock and rhododendron. It offers many good views. Blueberries are plentiful in season. Although rocky, the Trail is relatively level, with some moderate up-and-down stretches and occasional short, steep sections. The high point of the section—on the ridge north of Crater Lake—is 1,606 feet, and the lowest point is 935 feet at U.S. 206 in Culvers Gap.

This section has one important side trail—the 1.6-mile trail to Buttermilk Falls. Although rather steep in parts, the trail leads to a beautiful waterfall and is well worth the effort.

Maps—For route navigation, refer to Maps 5 and 6 with this guide. For area detail, refer to the following USGS 7½-minute topographic quadrangles: Culvers Gap, New Jersey–Pennsylvania; Newton West, New Jersey (small corner only); Flatbrookville, New Jersey–Pennsylvania. Other references are NY–NJ TC Trail Maps 16 and 17 (Kittatinny Trails).

Shelters and Campsites—This section has one shelter, Brink Road Shelter (see mile 3.6 below). Thru-hikers may camp along most of the Trail on the southern 10 miles of this section, subject to restrictions (see mile 4.7 below). No open fires are permitted. Bear activity is high in this section, so use bear boxes at the shelter, or, if tenting, hang food bags from a tree, using proper bear-bagging techniques.

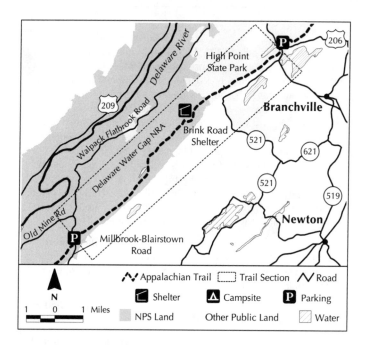

Appalachian Trail · Trail Section · Road
Shelter · Campsite · P Parking
NPS Land · Other Public Land · Water

N
1 0 1 Miles

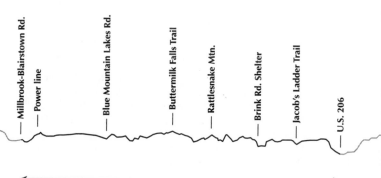

Millbrook-Blairstown Rd.

Power line

Blue Mountain Lakes Rd.

Buttermilk Falls Trail

Rattlesnake Mtn.

Brink Rd. Shelter

Jacob's Ladder Trail

U.S. 206

S   14.5 MILES   N

SECTION HIGHLIGHTS

Northern end of section →

A parking area is adjacent to the A.T., 0.3 mile north of the Trail crossing of U.S. 206, on Sunrise Mountain Road, just north of its intersection with County 636 (Upper North Shore Road). Registration at Stokes State Forest office is required for overnight parking; the office is 0.5 mile west on U.S. 206. A limited selection of groceries may be obtained at Worthington's Bakery, immediately west of the crossing. A grocery store is located on U.S. 206, 1.6 miles southeast of the crossing. Meals are available at a restaurant 0.1 mile west of the crossing. A hunting store, which sells freeze-dried foods and some camping equipment, is 0.2 mile west. A post office and a coin laundry are located in Branchville (ZIP Code 07826), 3.4 miles southeast of the Trail crossing on U.S. 206. Motels are located on U.S. 206, 2.5 miles east and 1.9 miles west of the Trail.

Stokes State Forest →

Camping is not permitted along the Trail on the northern 4.5 miles of this section, where it passes through Stokes State Forest, except at the Brink Road Shelter.

Acropolis Trail →

Leads 0.3 mile east, down to Culvers Lake and U.S. 206.

Jacobs Ladder Trail →

Leads 0.3 mile west to a woods road, which can be followed north to Kittatinny Lake, a residential area.

Brink Road →

Road access and parking are available west of the A.T.

Brink Road Shelter →

Built in 1970; 900 feet off A.T. on dirt road; accommodates 5; wooden floor; water from spring 350 feet beyond shelter on blue-blazed trail; privy on opposite side of road on blue-blazed trail. Bears are active around this shelter, so please use the bear box to store food overnight. Next shelter: north, 6.7 miles (Gren Anderson Shelter); south, 31.1 miles (Kirkridge Shelter in Pennsylvania).

N-S

TRAIL DESCRIPTION

0.0 The **northern end of section** is at the intersection of **14.5**
County 636 (Upper North Shore Road) with U.S. 206
at Culvers Gap (elev. 935 ft.) in **Stokes State Forest**.
Southbound hikers proceed east on U.S. 206 for a short
distance, then turn right and ascend. Northbound hikers
proceed north on the footpath from the northwest corner
of the intersection.

0.5 Cross under a power line (elev. 1,300 ft.) above Culvers **14.0**
Gap, with views to east over Culvers Lake toward Branchville, New Jersey. Just south of the power-line crossing,
cross a gravel road, route of the gold-and-dark-brown-
blazed **Acropolis Trail**.

0.8 Reach a clearing at the crest of the ridge. The Trail makes **13.7**
a right-angle turn, with views to the east of U.S. 206 and
Culvers Gap below.

1.2 Reach a viewpoint in a large, cleared area. Culvers Lake **13.3**
and U.S. 206 are visible to the northeast, and the Culver
Fire Tower is visible looking north along the Trail.

1.9 The blue/gray-blazed **Jacobs Ladder Trail** descends to **12.6**
the west.

2.1 An unmarked side trail leads east to an overlook of Lake **12.4**
Owassa.

3.0 Pass a field of rocks and boulders to the east of the Trail. **11.5**

3.2 Please sign the Trail register on a tree east of the Trail. **11.3**

3.6 Cross dirt **Brink Road**. A blue-blazed trail leads west 900 **10.9**
feet to the **Brink Road Shelter**.

SECTION HIGHLIGHTS

Wallpack Valley →

A section of the Delaware Valley in Sussex County, New Jersey, near Wallpack Bend, where the river makes a dramatic S-curve as it flows toward the Delaware Water Gap. One source calls Wallpack a corruption of the word "Wahlpeck," which in the Lenape language meant a whirlpool in the water—apparently a compound of the words for "hole" and "pool."

Pocono Plateau →

The geology of Pennsylvania's Pocono Plateau, west of the "Ridge and Valley Province" that the A.T. follows, is mostly shales and sandstone. Its mountains range in height from 1,900 to 2,200 feet above sea level. Long a popular resort and recreation area, the Poconos are full of gorges and cascades—more than a third of the state's 75 major waterfalls are there. Glacial action during the last Ice Age marked the land dramatically, scouring lakes, leaving boulder fields, and revealing a rich collection of fossils.

Stokes State Forest →

Covering 15,482 acres along Kittatinny Mountain, the state forest was purchased in 1907 and named after Gov. Edward C. Stokes, who donated 500 acres to the people of New Jersey. Old-growth forest along the ridge was cut for timber by the mid-ninteenth century, but the poor soil there made the area mostly unsuitable for farming. The park office is about 0.5 mile northwest of the northern end of the section, just north of U.S. 206

Camping →

Long-distance hikers may camp along the A.T. in the Delaware Water Gap National Recreation Area, from about 1.0 mile south of Brink Road to Millbrook–Blairstown Road, subject to the following conditions: Camping is permitted only in areas that are more than 0.5 mile from road accesses or the boundaries of the national recreation area. No camping is permitted from 0.5 mile south of Blue Mountain Lakes Road to 1.0 mile north of Crater Lake (Lake Success), where the Wallpack Township-Stillwater Township boundary crosses the

N-S

| TRAIL DESCRIPTION |

4.3 Reach a cleared area on the crest of the ridge, with sweep- **10.2**
ing views over the **Wallpack Valley** and the **Pocono Plateau** in Pennsylvania to the west.

4.7 Cross the boundary between **Stokes State Forest** and the **9.8**
Delaware Water Gap National Recreation Area, marked
by a sign. (See note at left about **camping** along the Trail
here.) The Trail intersects with a dirt road. Southbound
hikers turn left onto the dirt road. Northbound hikers turn
right, leaving the dirt road, and continue on a footpath.

5.0 The Trail intersects with a dirt road leading to the sum- **9.5**
mit of Bird Mountain (elev. 1,497 ft.). Southbound hikers
turn left, leaving the dirt road, and continue on a rocky
footpath, bypassing the summit. Northbound hikers turn
right onto the dirt road. Just north of the intersection, a
short, unmarked path to the west leads to a west-facing
viewpoint.

5.5 Cross a stream on rocks (elev. 1,260 ft.) between Bird and **9.0**
Rattlesnake mountains.

S-N

Trail (about 3.5 miles north of Blue Mountain Lakes Road). Where camping is permitted, hikers must camp not more than 100 feet from the Trail and at least 200 feet from other campsites. Camping is prohibited within 100 feet of any stream or water source, and any single campsite is limited to 10 persons.

Delaware Water Gap National Recreation Area →
The largest federal recreation area in the eastern United States, this 70,000-acre preserve extends along 40 miles of the Delaware River in Pennsylvania and New Jersey. See page 212 below.

Rattlesnake Mountain →
The geology of the mountains here is mostly Shawangunk conglomerates, which are more resistant to weathering than the shales of surrounding valleys that have eroded around them.

Buttermilk Falls Trail →
Hikers descend about 1,000 feet to the base of Buttermilk Falls. The first part of the trail is quite steep, but, after about 0.3 mile, the grade moderates. A dirt road, the route of the unmarked Woods Road Trail, is crossed at 0.5 mile. At 1.5 miles, after a short but very steep descent, the trail crosses a stream and arrives at the top of the falls. Wooden viewing platforms afford excellent views of the falls-the highest waterfall in New Jersey. The trail then descends to the base of the falls via a series of wooden steps and boardwalks, ending at Mountain Road at 1.6 miles.

Hemlock Pond Trail →
Leads west 0.4 mile to 15-acre Hemlock Pond, a scenic pond and popular fishing spot.

Crater Lake →
Early in the last century, 16-acre Crater Lake was a popular summer-cottage colony. The cottages were all razed by the federal government when it acquired the land in the 1960s and 1970s. Parking is available near the lake.

N-S	

> TRAIL DESCRIPTION

5.8	Reach a rock outcrop marking the summit of **Rattlesnake Mountain** (elev. 1,492 ft.), with views to the west of the **Wallpack Valley** and **Pocono Plateau.**	8.7
6.2	At the base of a descent, cross a stream on logs. Just north of the stream, a blue-blazed side trail leads east to a water source.	8.3
6.7	An unmarked trail to the west leads to a western-facing viewpoint from slanted rock slabs, with pitch pines growing from the cracks in the rocks.	7.8
7.4	The Trail intersects with a gravel road. Southbound hikers follow the A.T. along the road. Northbound hikers continue ahead on a footpath, as the road curves to the east.	7.1
7.7	The blue-blazed **Buttermilk Falls Trail** leads west, descending in 1.6 miles to Buttermilk Falls, a dependable water source, and ending at Mountain Road.	6.8
8.5	The orange-blazed **Hemlock Pond Trail** intersects on the west side of the A.T.	6.0
8.8	A blue-blazed side trail leads east 150 feet to a viewpoint overlooking **Crater Lake**. Fifty feet south of the side trail, the A.T. intersects with a gravel road. Southbound hikers turn right off the gravel road, and, in 250 feet, reach a viewpoint to the west. Northbound hikers follow the road for the next 1.4 miles.	5.7

Harding Lake Rock Shelter →
Excavated in the 1940s, this prehistoric site may be hard to make
out without a trained eye. Archaeology indicates that it served as a
home to groups of native-American hunters 5,000 years ago.

Blue Mountain Lakes Road →
Vehicle access is available only from the west. Parking is available
both 150 feet east and 150 feet west of the Trail crossing. Formerly
known as Flatbrookville Road, it leads west to Wallpack Bend (see
mile 4.3 above) on the Delaware River. The Blue Mountain Lakes
area, with many miles of old roads, is a popular area for mountain-
biking and winter cross-country skiing.

N-S

| | TRAIL DESCRIPTION | |

8.9 The Trail traverses the face of a steep escarpment. **Harding Lake Rock Shelter** (not a Trail shelter) is on the west side of the Trail.   **5.6**

9.3 Pass a swamp to the east of the Trail.   **5.2**

9.5 The Trail crosses the steep face of a smooth rock.   **5.0**

10.5 Please sign the Trail register to the west of the Trail.   **4.0**

10.6 Reach paved **Blue Mountain Lakes Road.** Southbound hikers turn west and follow the road for 100 feet, then turn south along a dirt road, which the A.T follows for the next 1.6 miles. Northbound hikers turn east at the paved road and follow it for 100 feet, then turn north into the woods. A water pump (tested) is 100 feet south of the road crossing, on the west side of the Trail.   **3.9**

10.9 An unmarked woods road leads east 125 feet to a viewpoint over Fairview Lake and the New Jersey Highlands.   **3.6**

11.3 A clearing to the east of the Trail provides a view of Fairview Lake below.   **3.2**

12.2 The A.T. intersects with a dirt road. Southbound hikers turn left onto a footpath. Northbound hikers continue north along the dirt road, which the A.T. follows for the next 1.6 miles.   **2.3**

12.8 A red-and-white-blazed trail descends to the east over private property to Camp No-Be-Bo-Sco (Northern New Jersey Council, Boy Scouts of America).   **1.7**

13.6 A short side trail on the east side of the A.T. leads to an east-facing viewpoint, with Sand Pond of Camp No-Be-Bo-Sco visible directly below.   **0.9**

S-N

Wallpack Valley, Pocono Plateau →
See mile 4.3 above.

Beaver pond →
Beavers, like bears, have returned in force to the national recreation area. Because trapping is not permitted here, few natural predators threaten them. As their habitat outside the protected zone shrinks, they threaten to overpopulate the area, flooding meadows of endangered plants and drowning woodlands. A grown beaver downs up to 300 trees each year. Beaver ponds eventually give way to swamps and meadows, providing a rich habitat for other animals.

Millbrook–Blairstown Road →
The Trail crosses Millbrook–Blairstown Road, 6.2 miles northwest of Blairstown and 1.1 miles southeast of Millbrook Village, a collection of historical buildings. Parking is available at the Trail crossing.

Southern end of section →
Groceries, meals, a coin laundry, and a post office (ZIP Code 07825) are available in Blairstown. No public transportation is available.

N-S

| TRAIL DESCRIPTION |

13.7 Cross under a power line and follow the power line across **0.8**
the ridge, with views to west of the **Wallpack Valley** and
Pocono Plateau.

14.0 Crosses a wooden bridge over the outlet of a **beaver** **0.5**
pond.

14.4 The Trail intersects with the paved **Millbrook–Blairstown** **0.1**
Road. Southbound hikers turn left and follow the road
east. Northbound hikers turn right, leaving the road, and
enter the woods on a footpath.

14.5 **Southern end of section**. The Trail intersects with paved **0.0**
Millbrook-Blairstown Road. Southbound hikers turn right,
leaving the paved road, and continue on a woods road
(New Jersey Section Six below). Northbound hikers turn
left and follow the paved road.

S-N

Millbrook–Blairstown Road to Delaware Water Gap

13.7 MILES

The Trail in this section follows the ridge of the Kittatinny Mountains. At the southern end, it crosses the Delaware River at the Delaware Water Gap. The northern part of this section lies within the boundaries of the Delaware Water Gap National Recreation Area, and the southern part passes through Worthington State Forest. The Trail climbs to the Catfish Fire Tower (elev. 1,565 ft.) and it passes Sunfish Pond, a glacial lake, near its southern end. Beautiful views are to be had from both sides of the ridge. The southern part of the route runs along Dunnfield Creek and reaches the Delaware River at the Delaware Water Gap, crossing the river on the Interstate-80 bridge (elev. 350 ft.).

Maps—For route navigation, refer to Map 6 with this guide. For area detail, refer to the following USGS 7½-minute topographic quadrangles: Flatbrookville, New Jersey–Pennsylvania; Bushkill, Pennsylvania–New Jersey; Portland, New Jersey–Pennsylvania; Stroudsburg, Pennsylvania–New Jersey. Other references are NY–NJ TC Trail Maps 15 and 16 (Kittatinny Trails-South).

Shelters and Campsites—No shelters are located in this section. Camping is permitted along the Trail in the national recreation area (see mile 0.0 below) and at Worthington State Forest's Backpacker Site (mile 9.1 below); camping is otherwise prohibited. Camping is also available at the Mohican Outdoor Center (mile 3.4 below) and at a developed campground on the Delaware River, accessed *via* the blue-blazed Douglas Trail that departs from the A.T. at mile 9.1 below (fee charged).

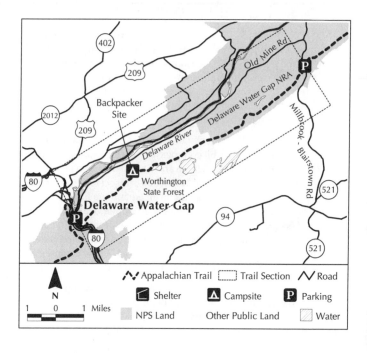

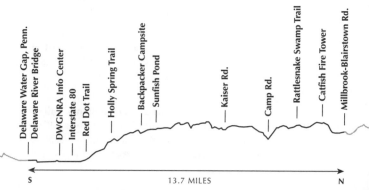

SECTION HIGHLIGHTS

Northern end of section →

Parking is available at the Trail crossing. Groceries, meals, a coin laundry, and a post office (ZIP Code 07825) are available in Blairstown, New Jersey. No public transportation is available. The Trail crossing is 6.2 miles northwest of Blairstown and 1.1 miles southeast of Millbrook Village, a collection of historic buildings in the Delaware Gap National Recreation Area.

Camping →

Camping by long-distance hikers is permitted in the Delaware Water Gap National Recreation Area (from about two miles north of Sunfish Pond to the northern terminus of this section), subject to the following restrictions: Camping is permitted only in areas more than 0.5 mile from road crossings or the boundaries of the national recreation area. Hikers must camp not more than 100 feet from the Trail and at least 200 feet from other campsites. Camping is prohibited within 100 feet of any stream or water source, and any single campsite is limited to 10 persons. No open fires are permitted.

Rattlesnake Swamp Trail →

Leaves the gravel road 0.1 mile west of the A.T. and leads south 2.0 miles to a trail to Catfish Pond and Mohican Outdoor Center, then continues for 0.5 mile, rejoining the A.T. at mile 2.0 below.

Catfish Fire Tower →

Built in 1922, this sixty-foot-high tower offers splendid, 360-degree views of the Kittatinnny range.

Rattlesnake Swamp Trail →

Leads 0.5 mile west to Catfish Pond and Mohican Outdoor Center, then 2.0 miles north to the fire tower road, near the A.T. at mile 0.4 above.

Camp Road and Coppermines Trail →

Camp Road leads west 0.3 mile to Mohican Outdoor Center (MOC) and Catfish Pond, where water, campsites, and lodging are available. Camping is free for thru-hikers; all others are charged a nominal

N-S

TRAIL DESCRIPTION

0.0 **Northern end of section.** Trail intersects with paved   **13.7**
Millbrook-Blairstown Road. Southbound hikers proceed
south on a gravel road (which leads to the Catfish Fire
Tower). Northbound hikers turn left and proceed west on
paved Millbrook-Blairstown Road. See note on **camping**
at left.

0.4 A.T. intersects with the gravel fire-tower road. Southbound   **13.3**
hikers turn left, leaving the gravel road, and ascend
through a rhododendron thicket. Northbound hikers turn
right onto the gravel road. The Rattlesnake Spring is 50 feet
west of the A.T. along the fire-tower road, between the A.T.
and the trailhead where the orange-blazed **Rattlesnake
Swamp Trail** intersects with the gravel fire-tower road.

0.6 The Trail turns left and joins the gravel fire-tower road for   **13.1**
300 feet, then turns right and reenters the woods.

0.7 The Trail intersects with the gravel fire-tower road. South-   **13.0**
bound hikers turn right onto the gravel road. Northbound
hikers turn left and descend, leaving the gravel road.

1.0 Reach **Catfish Fire Tower** (elev. 1,565 ft.).   **12.7**

2.0 Orange-blazed **Rattlesnake Swamp Trail** intersects on the   **11.7**
west side of the A.T., south of open ledges with views to
the east.

3.4 Cross dirt **Camp Road** (formerly known as Mohican Road).   **10.3**
Just south of road crossing, the Trail crosses Yards Creek, a
water source, and red-blazed **Coppermines Trail** intersects
on the west side of the A.T.

4.0 Open areas to the east of the Trail, suitable for camping,   **9.7**
provide limited views.

S-N

> ### SECTION HIGHLIGHTS
>
> fee. The Coppermines Trail leads 1.0 mile west to Coppermine Falls and 1.0 mile farther to historic Old Mine Road, with access to the Delaware River and a parking area.
>
> #### Lower Yards Creek Reservoir →
> Visible east of the A.T., this "pumped storage" generating station uses the steep terrain to meet peak power demands. Water is pumped to the upper lake (mile 6.8 below) when demand is low, and then rushes back to the lower lake when demand is high, turning three generators that produce 140 megawatts each.
>
> #### Kaiser Road Trail →
> The grassed-over woods road is named for the Kaiser family, who owned land and mineral rights in the area. To the west, it leads 1.5 miles to Old Mine Road, where parking is available.
>
> #### Kaiser Road →
> Leads southeast 0.8 mile down Kittatinny Ridge to Yards Creek Reservoir area and a Boy Scout camp. A spring is located 0.3 mile down the slope from the trail junction.
>
> #### Worthington State Forest →
> Named after C.C. Worthington, a prominent New Jersey industrialist and financier who bought the tract in 1890 from the DePue family, which acquired the lands in the early 1700s. Before conveying it to the state, Worthington maintained the 6,200 acres as Buckwood Park, a game preserve, and was an early practitioner of modern methods of reforestation.
>
> #### Upper Yards Creek Reservoir →
> Access to the reservoir is not permitted, because rapidly changing water levels from the pumped storage process (see mile 4.9 above) make it dangerous.
>
> #### Garvey Springs Trail →
> Leads 600 feet to Garvey Springs, a seasonal water source, and continues 1.2 miles to River Road (Old Mine Road).

N-S

TRAIL DESCRIPTION

4.9	Pass views to the east of the Trail of storage ponds for the **Lower Yards Creek Reservoir**.	**8.8**
5.3	The blue-blazed **Kaiser Road Trail** intersects on the west side of the A.T.	**8.4**
5.6	**Kaiser Road** intersects on the east side of the A.T.	**8.1**
5.8	Pass the boundary between Delaware Water Gap National Recreation Area and **Worthington State Forest**, marked by signs.	**7.9**
6.0	Reach a large pile of rocks at an excellent viewpoint to the east, with **Lower Yards Creek Reservoir** and storage ponds for the pumped-storage generating station visible below.	**7.7**
6.1	A power line crosses the Trail, with views on both sides of the ridge.	**7.6**
6.8	Cross a brook near **Upper Yards Creek Reservoir**.	**6.9**
7.7	The yellow-blazed **Garvey Springs Trail** intersects on the west side of the A.T. and leads to a spring.	**6.0**

Garvey Spring

S-N

| SECTION HIGHLIGHTS |

Turquoise Trail →
Leads 0.4 mile along the north shore of Sunfish Pond to Sunfish Pond Fire Road.

Sunfish Pond →
No camping or swimming is permitted along the shores of this pond, formed by the scooping action of glaciers during the last Ice Age, 10,000 years ago. It is the southernmost glacial pond on the Trail.

Sunfish Drainage Trail →
An unmarked trail that leads steeply down, next to the drainage channel from Sunfish Pond, west 1.0 mile to Rockcores Trail (named after the rock cores left along it during surveying for the proposed—but never built—Tocks Island Dam, which would have created an impoundment along the Delaware River (see note, mile 9.7 below).

Sunfish Pond Fire Road →
This fire road runs along the east side of the pond, leading to the east face of Kittatinny Mountain. Near the A.T. junction, the green-blazed Dunnfield Creek Trail leads 3.5 miles south along the Dunfield Creek ravine, passing the site of a nineteenth-century sawmill, and intersects with A.T. at mile 11.8 below.

Backpacker Site →
No water is available at this campsite, and camping is subject to the following restrictions: No ground fires are permitted. Camping is limited to one night. Groups are limited to 10 persons.

Douglas Trail →
Leads 1.7 miles to a developed campground in Worthington State Forest along the Delaware River. It is named after U.S. Supreme Court Justice William O. Douglas, an ardent conservationist and A.T. "2,000-miler" who campaigned against the proposed Tocks Island Dam. In 1962, Congress authorized construction the dam which would have flooded much of the Wallpack Valley along the Delaware River. Several years later, the Delaware Water Gap National Recreation Area was established to provide recreational facilities at

N-S

| | TRAIL DESCRIPTION | |

7.8 The **Turquoise Trail** (blazed "turquoise") intersects on the east side of the A.T. Two hundred feet to the south, the A.T. reaches the northeast end of **Sunfish Pond**. **5.9**

8.0 Follow a rocky footpath along the northwest shore of **Sunfish Pond**, passing interesting rock sculptures east of the Trail. **5.7**

8.2 Cross the outlet to the pond, and the **Sunfish Drainage Trail**. **5.5**

8.5 Pass the southwest end of **Sunfish Pond** (elev. 1,382 ft.), where **Sunfish Pond Fire Road** meets the A.T. The monument on the west side of the Trail notes that the Sunfish Pond Natural Area has been designated a registered natural landmark. Southbound hikers begin 1,000-foot descent along an old carriage route to the Delaware Water Gap. **5.2**

9.1 Pass **Backpacker Site** (no water). The blue-blazed **Douglas Trail** intersects on the west side of the A.T. Southbound hikers turn left, leaving the road, and continue on a rocky footpath. Northbound hikers turn right onto the old carriage road. **4.6**

9.7 A grassy road which intersects on the west side of the A.T. leads west to the **Douglas Trail**. **4.0**

10.0 An open area to the east of the Trail provides views of Kittatinny Ridge, which the A.T. follows for many miles on both sides of the river. **3.7**

S-N

the proposed lake. Strong opposition to the dam by Douglas, along with conservation groups, A.T. proponents, and local residents, resulted in the project being repeatedly postponed; the dam was formally deauthorized in 1992.

Beulahland Trail →
Leads west to Farview Parking Area on River Road (Old Mine Road) in 1.3 miles.

Holly Spring Trail →
Leads 0.2 mile east to Holly Spring, a water source (may fail in dry weather), and continues for another 0.2 mile to the Dunnfield Creek Trail.

Blue Dot Trail →
Leads east 1.8 miles to the summit of Mt. Tammany, overlooking the Delaware Water Gap. It can be combined with the A.T. and Red Dot Trail (mile 12.4 below) to make a scenic loop.

Dunnfield Creek Trail →
Leads north 3.1 miles to the Sunfish Pond Fire Road at mile 8.5 above, near its junction with the A.T. at Sunfish Pond.

Delaware Water Gap National Recreation Area →
The largest federal recreation area in the eastern United States, this 70,000-acre preserve extends along 40 miles of the Delaware River in Pennsylvania and New Jersey. It was originally planned as part of a massive hydroelectric dam project; the recreation area would have been along the shores of the lake. Many dwellings were destroyed and hundreds of families displaced in the farming country and hillsides along the river before plans for the dam were shelved, after intense opposition. Beginning in the late 1980s, the National Park Service began developing beaches, roads, boat launches, picnic areas, and trails in the area and preserving the remaining historical structures. The A.T. runs through a section of the recreation area on the Kittatinny Ridge.

N-S

TRAIL DESCRIPTION

Sunfish Pond

10.7	The yellow-blazed **Beulahland Trail** intersects on the west side of the A.T., and the red-blazed **Holly Spring Trail** intersects on the east side of the A.T.	**3.0**
11.8	The blue-blazed **Blue Dot Trail** and the green-blazed **Dunnfield Creek Trail** intersect sharply on the east side of the A.T.	**1.9**
12.1	The Trail makes a right-angle turn. Southbound hikers turn left, leaving an old carriage road. Northbound hikers begin a 1,000-foot ascent along the old carriage route to **Sunfish Pond**. Two hundred feet to the south, the Trail crosses a wooden bridge over Dunnfield Creek.	**1.6**
12.2	Reach a pump, a tested water source, at the northern end of the parking area.	**1.5**
12.3	The southern end of the parking area (elev 350 ft.), is marked by a sign, "Dunnfield Creek Natural Area." Southbound hikers turn left along a paved road and then, in 250 feet, make a right turn at an underpass, and go under Interstate-80. Northbound hikers turn right into the parking area.	**1.4**

S-N

Delaware Water Gap →

Meals, groceries, and other supplies may be obtained in the village, and packages can be mailed at the post office (ZIP Code 18327). Motels are available, and the Presbyterian Church of the Moountain provides an information center and a hostel for long-distance hikers. Limited bus service to New York City and to other points is available *via* Martz Trailways, (800) 233-8604.

Southern end of section →

The Trail crosses the Delaware River on the Interstate-80 toll bridge at the Delaware Water Gap. No parking is available at the Pennsylvania side of the Delaware River bridge; however, ample parking is provided at the Delaware Water Gap National Recreation Area Information Center on the New Jersey side of the bridge, 1.2 miles from the southern terminus of the section. Additional parking is available at the Dunnfield Creek Natural Area, 1.4 miles from the southern end of the section, where the Trail leaves paved roads and begins its climb of the Kittatinny Ridge. Motorists approaching from the east should exit I-80 before crossing the bridge, at the sign marked "Rest Area." Those coming from the west should take the first exit after crossing the bridge into New Jersey.

N-S

TRAIL DESCRIPTION

12.4　Pass the southern end of the underpass. Southbound hikers　**1.3**
turn right and continue along a paved road parallel to I-80.
Northbound hikers turn left at the underpass, go under I-
80, then turn left at the northern end of the underpass and
continue along a paved road. (The Red Dot Trail intersects
here. It leads 1.5 miles to the summit of Mt. Tammany and
can be combined with the A.T. and the Blue Dot Trail (mile
11.8 above) to make a 5.9-mile loop.)

12.5　Pass a Trail register (please sign) and **Delaware Water Gap**　**1.2**
National Recreation Area Information Center on east side
of the Trail. The center offers water, restrooms, picnic area,
boat launching, and parking.

13.0　Reach the northern (compass-east) end of the Interstate-　**0.7**
80 bridge over the Delaware River. Southbound hikers
continue across bridge into Pennsylvania. Northbound
hikers continue along the service road on the east side
of Interstate 80.

13.7　The **southern end of section** is in the village of **Delaware**　**0.0**
Water Gap, Pennsylvania, just south of the toll plaza,
where a dead-end street comes in on the south side of Interstate 80. Southbound hikers turn left onto the dead-end
street (see *The Appalachian Trail Guide to Pennsylvania*).
Northbound hikers turn right onto a sidewalk along Interstate 80 and cross the bridge over the Delaware River.

S-N

Suggested Day-Trips

Because the Appalachian Trail in New York and New Jersey is crisscrossed by many roads and side trails, it's an ideal area for shorter day-hikes, loops, and out-and-back walks, especially for those hikers who aren't looking for an overnight or long-distance backpacking experience. This chapter briefly describes some possible day-hikes in the area covered by this guidebook.

For more options, and greater detail, we suggest you consult the trail descriptions published by the New York–New Jersey Trail Conference in the *New York Walk Book, New Jersey Walk Book,* and *Harriman Trails: A Guide and History.* For maps, see the A.T. maps that accompany this guidebook and maps for Harriman and Bear Mountain state parks, North Jersey Trails, East Hudson Trails, and Kittatinny Trails, published by the NY–NJ TC. See page 274 for ordering information.

Please see "Questions and Answers about the Appalachian Trail" (page 220 below) for information on what to pack on a day trip.

Connecticut Section Five (New York Section One)
Indian Rocks—Climb to a fine overlook to the east, over the Housatonic River and its valley. One option begins at the northern end of the section at Conn. 341: Ascend southbound from Mt. Algo to Indian Rocks, and return—a 7.6-mile round-trip. The other option leaves from the parking area at Bulls Bridge: Hike north to Schaghticoke Road, then ascend Schaghticoke Mountain to Indian Rocks, and return, an 8.2-mile round-trip.

New York Section Three
Dover Oak to West Mountain—Begin at the massive Dover Oak, on County 20, near Pawling, N.Y, and climb south to an overlook on West Mountain, with views south over Dutchess County. From the Dover Oak, this is a 2.0-mile round-trip.

New York Section Four
Depot Hill Road to Mt. Egbert—Begin at Grape Hollow Road, at the foot of Depot Hill, and ascend across swamps, fields, and old homesteads to a good view from Mt. Egbert. From Grape Hollow Road, hiking north, this is a 4.8-mile round-trip.

New York Section Six
Canopus Lake to Shenandoah Mountain—This hike leads from a popular lakeside spot in Fahnestock State Park to a fine view from the open summit of Shenandoah Mountain. Beginning at N.Y. 301 and hiking north, it is an 8.4-mile round-trip.

New York Section Eight
Denning Hill—A view of the Manhattan skyline is possible from Denning Hill, the destination of a hike that leads north from U.S. 9 and N.Y. 403. The round-trip distance is 5.0 miles.

New York Section Ten
Bear Mountain Loop—Beginning at the Bear Mountain Inn and hiking south, this route leads to a fine view from the Perkins Memorial Tower atop Bear Mountain. By combining the A.T. route with the 2.6-mile Major Welch Trail (blazed red), hikers can take a 5.0-mile loop to the mountaintop and back.

New York Section Eleven
Elk Pen to the Lemon Squeezer—This short route takes hikers over Green Pond Mountain, past scenic Island Pond, to the famous Lemon Squeezer, a challenging cranny between glacial rocks. Hiking north from the Elk Pen parking area on Arden Valley Road (near N.Y. 17), the round-trip distance is 4.0 miles. An alternate return route *via* the Arden-Surebridge Trail would be a 5.5-mile round-trip.

New York Section Twelve
Buchanan Mountain—Hiking south from East Mombasha Road, this short, steep route leads past several viewpoints to the summit of Buchanan Mountain. The round-trip is 1.6 miles.

Mombasha High Point—In clear weather, a fine view of the Manhattan skyline is the reward of this hike, which takes you north from Lakes Road, past Fitzgerald Falls, to Mombasha High Point. Round-trip distance is 4.6 miles.

New York Section Thirteen and New Jersey Section One

Prospect Rock—A fine view of Greenwood Lake and a glimpse of the Manhattan skyline are to be had from Prospect Rock. This hike begins by climbing the State Line Trail from N.Y. 210, opposite the Greenwood Lake Marina, 1.2 miles to the A.T., at the state line, and then north 0.4 mile to Prospect Rock. Round-trip distance is 3.2 miles.

New Jersey Section One

Wawayanda Mountain—This long hike leads from the headquarters of Wawayanda State Park along a blue-blazed trail to the A.T. and from there south to Pinwheel's Vista, on Wawayanda Mountain, with fine views of the Shawangunks and Catskills, Vernon Valley, Pochuck Mountain, and the Kittatinny Ridge. Round-trip distance is 9.0 miles.

New Jersey Section Two

Pochuck Quagmire—This short, mostly level walk takes hikers along a scenic boardwalk and suspension bridge extending more than half a mile over Pochuck Creek and its surrounding wetlands. From the parking area at Canal Road, a hike south to the far side of the swamp and back has a round-trip distance of 2.6 miles.

Wallkill Flats—From the parking area at Oil City Road, this mostly flat loop hike leads around the Wallkill National Wildlife Refuge, where a 2.5-mile circuit on the A.T. and the Liberty Loop Trail skirts an old sod farm, now home to a dazzling array of bird life.

New Jersey Section Three

High Point—From the state park headquarters on N.J. 23, follow the A.T. north 1.2 miles, past the observation platform, to the red-and-green-blazed Monument Trail, which leads west to the monument. Good views are available from the platform and the monument. Round-trip distance is 2.8 miles.

New Jersey Section Five
Rattlesnake Mountain—Follow the A.T. north from Blue Mountain Lakes Road, reaching a good viewpoint on Rattlesnake Mountain, with vistas looking north and west. Round-trip distance is 9.6 miles.

New Jersey Section Six
Sunfish Pond—This long hike leads from the parking area in the Dunnfield Creek Natural Area of Delaware Water Gap National Recreation Area north and uphill to Sunfish Pond, a spectacular glacial pond. Round-trip distance is 7.4 miles. An alternative 6.9-mile loop route involves following the green-blazed Dunnfield Creek Trail up or down the mountain.

Mt. Tammany Loop—This hike combines the A.T., Red Dot, and Blue Dot trails in a 5.9-mile loop. See page 215 above.

Fitzgerald Falls

Questions and Answers
about the Appalachian Trail

Preparation

What should I carry?

The A.T. is enjoyable to hike, but inexperienced hikers—even those just out for an hour or two—can quickly find themselves deep in the woods, on steep terrain, and in wet, chilly conditions. Carrying a basic "kit" helps hikers cope with such situations.

Packing for a day-hike is relatively simple:

> Map and compass (learn to use them first!)
> Water (at least 1 quart, and 2-3 on longer hikes in hot weather)
> Warm clothing and rain gear
> Food (including extra high-energy snacks)
> Trowel (to bury human waste) and toilet paper
> First-aid kit, with blister treatments
> Whistle (three blasts is the international signal for help)
> Garbage bag (to carry out trash)

On longer hikes, especially in remote or rugged terrain, add:

> Flashlight (with extra batteries and bulb)
> Heavy-duty garbage bag (emergency shelter or to insulate
>   a hypothermia victim)
> Sharp knife
> Fire starter (a candle, for instance) and waterproof matches

If you're backpacking and plan to camp out, we suggest you consult a good "how-to" book for details about what to carry or talk to an experienced hiker. Although we don't have room here to discuss gear in detail, most A.T. backpackers carry the following items, in addition to the day-hike checklist. Some of the items can be shared with a partner to lighten the load:

Shelter (a tent or tarp)
Lightweight pot, cooking utensils
Stove (a small backpacking model, with fuel)
Medium-sized backpack (big "expedition-size" packs
      are usually overkill)
A pack cover or plastic bag (to keep gear dry in rainy weather)
Sleeping pad (to insulate you from the cold ground)
Sleeping bag of appropriate warmth for the season
Food and clothing
Rope or cord (to hang your food at night)
Water filter, iodine tablets, or another method of treating water

Where can I park?
Park in designated areas. Many of them will be indicated in the Trailhead entries for this guidebook and may be marked on Trail maps. If you leave your car overnight unattended, however, you risk theft or vandalism. Many hikers avoid this worry by arranging for a "shuttle" to drop them off at a Trailhead or arranging to leave their car in the parking lot of a business located near the Trail; ask first, and offer to pay a little something to the business. Some sections of the Trail are served by public transportation. If you decide to park at a Trailhead, hide your property and valuables from sight, or better yet, leave them at home, so they do not inspire a thief to break in and steal them.

Using the Trail

Where and how do I find water?
Reliable natural water sources are listed in this guidebook; springs and streams are marked on most official A.T. maps. Most (though not all) shelters are near a reliable water source. Some springs and streams dry up during late summer and early fall.

Is the water safe to drink?
Water in the backcountry and in water sources along the A.T. can be contaminated by microorganisms, including *giardia lamblia* and others that cause diarrhea or stomach problems. We recommend that you treat all water, using a filter or purifier or water treatment tablets, or by boiling it.

Are there rest rooms?
Many A.T. shelters have privies, but usually you will need to "go in the woods." Proper disposal of human (and pet) waste is not only a courtesy to other hikers, but a vital Leave No Trace practice for maintaining healthy water supplies in the backcountry and an enjoyable hiking experience for others. No one should venture onto the A.T. without a trowel, used for digging a 6"–8" deep "cathole" to bury waste. Bury feces at least two hundred feet or seventy paces away from water, trails, or shelters. Use a stick to mix dirt with your waste, which hastens decomposition and discourages animals from digging it up. Used toilet paper should either be buried in your cathole or carried out in a sealed plastic bag. Hygiene products such as sanitary napkins should always be carried out.

Can I wash up in a mountain stream or spring?
Please don't. Carry water from the water source in a bottle or other container, and then wash your dishes, and yourself, well away from streams, springs, and ponds. Don't leave food scraps to rot in water sources, and don't foul them with products such as detergent, toothpaste, and human or animal waste.

Are bikes allowed on the Trail?
Only where the Appalachian Trail shares the route with the C&O Towpath in Maryland, the Virginia Creeper Trail in the vicinity of Damascus, Virginia, roads in towns, and on certain bridges. They are not permitted on most of the Trail.

Can I bring my dog?
Yes, except where dogs are prohibited (in Great Smoky Mountains National Park, Bear Mountain Zoo, and Baxter State Park). Dogs must be leashed on National Park Service Lands and on many state park and forest lands. ATC's World Wide Web site, <www.appalachiantrail. org>, offers details about hiking with dogs. Although dogs can be wonderful hiking companions, they can create many problems for other hikers and wildlife if you don't control them. If taken, they should not be allowed to run free; leashing at all times is strongly recommended. Keep dogs out of springs and shelters and away from other hikers, their food, and their gear. Not all dogs can stand the wear and tear of a long hike.

How about horses, llamas, or other pack stock?

Horses are not allowed on the A.T., except where the Appalachian Trail coincides for about three miles with the C&O Canal Towpath in Maryland and on about 50 percent of the A.T. in the Smokies (where, by law, the route is open for horses as a historical use). Llamas and other pack animals are not allowed on the A.T., which is designed, built, and maintained by hikers for foot travel. Pack animals may seriously damage the treadway, discourage volunteer maintenance efforts, and make the Trail experience less enjoyable for other hikers.

Are any fees required to hike the A.T.?

No. However, there are entrance fees to some of the national parks the Trail passes through, as well as parking fees and campsite fees in popular areas to help pay for maintenance costs.

Health and safety

Is the Trail a safe place?

In general, yes. But, like many other popular recreational activities, hiking on the A.T. is not without risk. Don't let the following discussion of potential dangers alarm you or discourage you from enjoying the Trail, but remember not to leave your common sense and intuition behind when you strap on your backpack.

In an emergency, how do I get help?

Much of the A.T. is within range of mobile phone systems, although signal reception is sometimes not good in gaps, hollows, and valleys; shelters are often located in such areas of poor reception. Emergency numbers are included in this guidebook, and on maps. If you don't have a phone or can't get through, the standard call for distress consists of three short calls, audible or visible, repeated at regular intervals. A whistle is particularly good for audible signals. Visible signals may include, in daytime, light flashed with a mirror or smoke puffs; at night, a flashlight or three small bright fires. Anyone recognizing such a signal should acknowledge with two calls—if possible, by the same method—then go to the distressed person to determine the nature of the emergency. Arrange for additional aid, if necessary.

Most of the A.T. is well-enough traveled that, if you are injured, you can expect to be found. However, if an area is remote and the weather is bad, fewer hikers will be on the Trail, especially after dark. As a rule, keep your pack with you, and, even in an emergency, don't leave marked trails and try to "bushwhack" out—you will be harder to find and are more likely to encounter dangerous terrain. If you must leave the Trail, study the guidebook or map carefully for the nearest place where people are likely to be and attempt to move in that direction. If it is necessary to leave a heavy pack behind, be sure to take essentials, in case your rescue is delayed. In bad weather, a night in the open without proper covering could be fatal.

What's the most dangerous aspect of hiking the A.T.?
Perhaps the most serious dangers are hypothermia (see page 226 below), a fall on slick rocks and logs, or a sprained or broken limb far from the nearest rescue squad or pay phone. It's also the best argument for hiking with a partner, who can get help in an emergency.

What sort of first-aid kit should I pack?
A basic kit to take care of bruises, scrapes, skinned knees, and blisters. The following kit weighs about a pound and occupies about a 3" x 6" x 9" space: Eight 4" x 4" gauze pads; four 3" x 4" gauze pads; five 2" bandages; ten 1" bandages; six alcohol prep pads; ten large butterfly closures; one triangular bandage (40"); two 3" rolls of gauze; twenty tablets of aspirin-free pain-killer; one 15' roll of 2" adhesive tape; one 3" Ace bandage; one 3" x 4" moleskin or other blister care products; three safety pins; one small scissors; one tweezers; personal medications as necessary

Will I encounter snakes?
Poisonous and nonpoisonous snakes are widespread along the Trail in warm weather, but they will usually be passive. Watch where you step and where you put your hands. Please, don't kill snakes! Some are federally protected under the Endangered Species Act.

What other creatures are problems for people?
Allergic reactions to bee stings can be a problem. Ticks, which carry Lyme disease, are also a risk; always check yourself for ticks daily. Poisonous

spiders are sometimes found at shelters and campsites. Mosquitoes and blackflies may plague you in some seasons. Porcupines, skunks, raccoons, and squirrels are quite common and occasionally raid shelters and well-established camping areas after dark, looking for food. Mice are permanent residents at most shelters and may carry diseases.

What about bears?

Black bears live along many parts of the Trail and are particularly common in Georgia, the Shenandoah and Great Smoky Mountains national parks, and parts of Pennsylvania and New Jersey. They are always looking for food. Bears that have lost their fear of humans may "bluff charge" to get you to drop food or a backpack. If you encounter a black bear, it will probably run away. If it does not, back away slowly, watching the bear but not making direct eye contact. Do not run away or play dead. If a bear attacks, fight for all you are worth. The best defense against bears is preparing and storing food properly. Cook and eat your meals away from your tent or shelter, so food odors do not linger. Hang your food, cookware, toothpaste, and personal-hygiene items in a sturdy bag from a strong tree branch at least ten feet off the ground and well away from your campsite.

Is poison ivy common along the A.T.?

Yes. It grows plentifully in the wild, particularly south of New England, and can be an annoyance during hiking season. If you have touched poison ivy, wash immediately with strong soap (but not with one containing added oil). If a rash develops in the next day or so, treat it with calamine lotion or Solarcaine. Do not scratch. If blisters become serious or the rash spreads to the eyes, see a doctor.

Will I catch a disease?

The most common illnesses encountered on the A.T. are water-borne, come from ingesting protozoa (such as *giardia lamblia*), and respond well to antibiotics. But, the Lyme-disease bacterium and other tick-borne illnesses are legitimate concerns, too; mosquito-borne illnesses such as the West Nile virus are less common in Trail states. Cases of rabies have been reported in foxes, raccoons, and other small animals; a bite is a serious concern, though instances of hikers being bitten are rare. One case of the dangerous rodent-borne disease hantavirus has been reported on the A.T.: avoid sleeping on mouse droppings (use a mat or tent) or handling mice. Treat your water, and wash your hands.

Will I encounter hazardous weather?

Walking in the open means you will be susceptible to sudden changes in the weather, and traveling on foot means that it may be hard to find shelter quickly. Pay attention to the changing skies. Sudden spells of "off-season" cold weather, hail, and even snow are common along many parts of the Trail. Winter-like weather often occurs in late spring or early fall in the southern Appalachians, Vermont, New Hampshire, and Maine. In the northern Appalachians, it can snow during any month of the year.

What are the most serious weather-related dangers?

Hypothermia, lightning, and heat exhaustion are all legitimate concerns. Don't let the fear of them ruin your hike, but take sensible precautions.

Hypothermia—A cold rain can be the most dangerous weather of all, because it can cause hypothermia (or "exposure") even when conditions are well above freezing. Hypothermia occurs when wind and rain chill the body so that its core temperature drops; death occurs if the condition is not caught in time. Avoid hypothermia by dressing in layers of synthetic clothing, eating well, staying hydrated, and knowing when to hole up in a warm sleeping bag in a tent or shelter. Cotton clothing, such as blue jeans, tends to chill you when it gets wet from rain or sweat; if the weather turns bad, cotton clothes increase your risk of hypothermia. Natural wool and artificial fibers such as nylon, polyester, and polypropylene all do a much better job of insulation in cold, wet weather. Remember that, when the wind blows, its "chill" effect can make you much colder than the temperature would lead you to suspect, especially if you're sweaty or wet.

Lightning—The odds of being struck by lightning are low, but an open ridge is no place to be during a thunderstorm. If a storm is coming, immediately leave exposed areas. Boulders, rocky overhangs, and shallow caves offer no protection from lightning, which may actually flow through

TEMPERATURE (°F)

WIND (mph)	40	35	30	25	20	15	10	5	0	-5	-10	-15	-20	-25	-30	-35	-40	-45
5	36	31	25	19	13	7	1	-5	-11	-16	-22	-28	-34	-40	-46	-52	-57	-63
10	34	27	21	15	9	3	-4	-10	-16	-22	-28	-35	-41	-47	-53	-59	-66	-72
15	32	25	19	13	6	0	-7	-13	-19	-26	-32	-39	-45	-51	-58	-64	-71	-77
20	30	24	17	11	4	-2	-9	-15	-22	-29	-35	-42	-48	-55	-61	-68	-74	-81
25	29	23	16	9	3	-4	-11	-17	-24	-31	-37	-44	-51	-58	-64	-71	-78	-84
30	28	22	15	8	1	-5	-12	-19	-26	-33	-39	-46	-53	-60	-67	-73	-80	-87
35	28	21	14	7	0	-7	-14	-21	-27	-34	-41	-48	-55	-62	-69	-76	-82	-89
40	27	20	13	6	-1	-8	-15	-22	-29	-36	-43	-50	-57	-64	-71	-78	-84	-91
45	26	19	12	5	-2	-9	-16	-23	-30	-37	-44	-51	-58	-65	-72	-79	-86	-93
50	26	19	12	4	-3	-10	-17	-24	-31	-38	-45	-52	-60	-67	-74	-81	-88	-95
55	25	18	11	4	-3	-11	-18	-25	-32	-39	-46	-54	-61	-68	-75	-82	-89	-97
60	25	17	10	3	-4	-11	-19	-26	-33	-40	-48	-55	-62	-69	-76	-84	-91	-98

30 min.   10 min.   5 minutes

FROSTBITE TIMES

Wind Chill (°F) = 35.74 + 0.6215T - 35.75($V^{0.16}$) + 0.4275T($V^{0.16}$)
Where, T= Air Temperature (°F) V= Wind Speed (mph)
National Weather Sevice and National Oceanic and Atmospheric Administration
Effective 11/01/01

them along the ground after a strike. Tents and convertible automobiles are no good, either. Sheltering in hard-roofed automobiles or large buildings is best, though they're rarely available to the hiker. Avoid tall structures, such as ski lifts, flagpoles, powerline towers, and the tallest trees, solitary rocks, or open hilltops. If you cannot enter a building or car, take shelter in a stand of smaller trees or in the forest. Avoid clearings. If caught in the open, crouch down on your pack or pad, or roll into a ball. If you are in water, get out. Disperse groups, so that not everyone is struck by a single bolt. Do not hold a potential lightning rod, such as a fishing pole or metal hiking pole.

Heat—Dry, hot summers are surprisingly common along the Trail, particularly in the Virginias and the mid-Atlantic. Water may be scarce on humid days, sweat does not evaporate well, and many hikers face the danger of heat stroke and heat exhaustion if they haven't taken proper precautions, such as drinking lots of water. Learn how to protect yourself from heat exhaustion.

Is crime a problem?

The Appalachian Trail is safer than most places, but a few crimes of violence have occurred. Awareness is one of your best lines of defense. Be aware of what you are doing, where you are, and to whom you are talking. Hikers looking out for each other can be an effective "community watch." Be prudent and cautious without allowing common sense to slip into paranoia. Remember to trust your gut—it's usually right. Other tips include the following:

- Don't hike alone. If you are by yourself and encounter a stranger who makes you feel uncomfortable, say you are with a group that is behind you. Be creative. If in doubt, move on. Even a partner is no guarantee of safety, however; pay attention to your instincts about other people.

- Leave your hiking itinerary and timetable with someone at home. Be sure your contacts and your family know your "Trail name," if you use one of those fanciful aliases common on the A.T. Check in regularly, and establish a procedure to follow if you fail to check in. On short hikes, provide your contacts with the numbers of the land-managing agencies for the area of your hike. On extended hikes, provide ATC's number.

- Be wary of strangers. Be friendly, but cautious. Don't tell strangers your plans. Avoid people who act suspiciously, seem hostile, or are intoxicated.

- Don't camp near roads.

- Dress conservatively to avoid unwanted attention.

- Don't carry firearms. They are prohibited on National Park Service lands and in most other areas without a permit, they could be turned against you or result in an accidental shooting, and they are extra weight.

■ Eliminate opportunities for theft. Don't bring jewelry. Hide your money. If you must leave your pack, hide it or leave it with someone trustworthy. Don't leave valuables or equipment (especially in sight) in vehicles parked at Trailheads.

■ Use the Trail registers (the notebooks stored at most shelters). Sign in using your given name, leave a note, and report any suspicious activities. If someone needs to locate you, or if a serious crime has been committed along the Trail, the first place authorities will look is in the registers.

■ Report any crime or harassment to the local authorities and ATC.

Trail history

Who was Benton MacKaye, and what was his connection to the Appalachian Trail?

He first published the idea. MacKaye (1879-1973) grew up in Shirley Center, Massachusetts, reading the work of American naturalists and poets and taking long walks in the mountains of Massachusetts and Vermont. MacKaye (which is pronounced like "sky") sometimes claimed that the idea for the A.T. was born one day when he was sitting in a tree atop Stratton Mountain in Vermont. But, after graduating from Harvard, he went to work in the new U.S. Forest Service and began carving out a niche as a profound thinker and an advocate for wilderness. By 1919, his radical ideas had led to him being edged out of the USFS, and he turned his attention to creating a new discipline that later came to be called "regional planning." His initial 1921 "project in regional planning" was a proposal for a network of work camps and communities in the mountains, all linked by a trail that ran from the highest point in New England to the highest point in the South. He called it the Appalachian Trail.

Why did he propose it?

MacKaye was convinced that the pace of urban and industrial life along the East Coast was harmful to people. He envisioned the A.T. as a path interspersed with planned wilderness communities where people could go to renew themselves. That idea never gained much traction, but the notion of a thousand-mile footpath in the mountains fired the imaginations of hikers and outdoorsmen from Maine to Georgia. Inspired by him, they began building trails and trying to connect them.

What was his connection to the Appalachian Trail Conference?

MacKaye was responsible for convening and organizing the first Appalachian Trail "conference" in Washington, D.C., in 1925. That gathering of hikers, foresters, and public officials embraced the goal of building the Trail. They established an organization, called the Appalachian Trail Conference, appointed MacKaye as its "field organizer," and named Major William Welch, manager of New York's Harriman Park, as its first chairman.

What happened next?

Some perfunctory scouting of routes took place. A few short sections were marked and connected. New trails were built in New York. Welch designed a logo and Trail markers. Committees met in a few northeastern states and talked about the idea. But, for several years, the idea didn't really go anywhere. MacKaye was much better at inspirational abstract thinking than practical organizing, and it soon became apparent that someone else was going to have to take the lead for the Trail to actually get built.

Who pushed the project forward?

Two men, retired Judge Arthur Perkins of Connecticut and admiralty lawyer Myron Avery of Washington, D.C. Perkins took the idea and ran with it, essentially appointing himself as the acting chairman of ATC in the late 1920s and recruiting Avery to lead the effort in the area around Washington. Both began vigorously proselytizing the idea of the Trail in 1928 and 1929, championing MacKaye's ideas to recruit volunteers, establishing hiking clubs up and down the coast, and actually going out to hike, clear brush, and mark paths themselves. As Perkins' health failed in the early 1930s, Avery took over, devoting incredible time, energy, and willpower to establishing a network of volunteers, developing clubs, working with the government, building the organization of the ATC, and setting the Trail's northern terminus at Katahdin in his native Maine. Avery remained chairman of ATC until 1952.

What was the relationship between MacKaye and Myron Avery?

They were cordial at first, but, by the mid-1930s, as Avery took charge of the Trail project, they quarreled over fundamental issues and visions of what the Trail should be. Avery was more interested in hiking and in connecting the sections of the Trail, while MacKaye was more interested in the Trail's role in promoting wilderness. MacKaye disassociated himself from the Conference in 1935 to found the Wilderness Society and was not closely involved with the Trail again until after Avery's death in 1952.

When was the Trail completed?

In 1937. It fell into disrepair during World War II, when Trail maintainers were unable to work on it, and parts of the route were lost, but, after the war a concerted effort was made to restore it, and it was once again declared complete in 1951.

What happened after it was completed?

It's useful to look at the Trail's history in three eras: the era of Trail-building, which lasted until the Trail was completed in 1937; the era of Trail protection, which lasted until 1968, when Congress made the A.T. a national scenic trail; and the era of management and promotion, which has lasted until the present day. The first era was dominated by personalities and focused on getting the thing built and blazed from one end to the other. The second era saw the growth of the clubs taking care of it, the growth of the Conference, the construction of shelters, and a continuing battle to keep the route open over the many hundreds of miles of private property that it crossed. The third era saw an explosion of the number of people hiking the A.T. as the government began buying land along the route to guarantee the permanence of the footpath and volunteers shifted their emphasis to the hard work of managing a part of the national park system.

How was the original Trail different from today's A.T.?

At first, the goal was simply to blaze a connected route. Often, this meant that the Trail led along old forest roads and other trails. Trail maintainers mostly just cleared brush and painted blazes. Today's Trail has mostly been moved off the old roads and onto new paths dug and reinforced especially for hikers. Today's route, though engineered much more elaborately, often requires more climbing, because it leads up the sides of many mountains that the old woods roads bypassed.

How do terms like "Trailway," "greenway," "buffer," and "viewshed" fit into this history?

The idea of a "Trailway" was first embraced by ATC in 1937. It meant that there was more to the Appalachian Trail than just the footpath. The "Trailway" referred to an area dedicated to the interests of those on foot, originally a mile on either side. In some cases, that came to mean a "buffer"—a legally protected area around the path that kept the sights and sounds of civilization, logging, and development away from the solitary hiker. In other cases, it meant a great deal more. It evolved into a notion of a "greenway," a broad swath of protected land through which the Trail ran. Crucial to the idea of a greenway was that of the "viewshed," the countryside visible from the Trail's high points. In the years since the A.T. became a national scenic trail, the Conference has worked to influence the development of surrounding areas so that the views from the Trail remain scenic, even when those views are of areas well outside the boundaries of the public Trail lands themselves.

When did Trail protection begin?

The notion of a protected zone was first formalized in an October 15, 1938, agreement between the National Park Service and the U.S. Forest Service for the promotion of an Appalachian Trailway through the relevant national parks and forests, extending one mile on each side of the Trail. Within this zone, no new parallel roads would be built or any other incompatible development allowed. Timber cutting would not be permitted within 200 feet of the Trail. Similar agreements, creating a zone one-quarter-mile in width, were signed with most states through which the Trail passes.

How were Trail lands identified?

Much of the Trail was already in national forests or national parks and state and local parks, but large portions were on private property, with the agreement of the property owners. In 1970, supplemental agreements under the 1968 National Trails Systems Act—among the National Park Service, the U.S. Forest Service, and the Appalachian Trail Conference—established the specific responsibilities of those organizations for initial mapping, selection of rights-of-way, relocations, maintenance, development, acquisition of land, and protection of a permanent Trail. Agreements also were signed between the Park Service and the various states, encouraging them to acquire and protect a right-of-way for the Trail outside federal land.

Why has complete protection taken so long?

Getting federal money appropriated was difficult, and not all property owners were willing to sell, which occasionally raised the specter of the government threatening to condemn land for the Trail—always a politically unpopular action. Slow progress of federal efforts and lack of initiative by some states led Congress to strengthen the National Trails System Act in an amendment known as the Appalachian Trail Bill, which was signed by President Jimmy Carter on March 21, 1978. The new legislation emphasized the need for protecting the Trail, including acquiring a corridor, and authorized $90 million for that purpose. More money was appropriated during the Reagan, Bush, and Clinton administrations. Today, 99 percent of the Trail runs along public lands.

What is the relationship between the A.T. and the government, the Conference, and the clubs?

In 1984, the Interior Department delegated the responsibility for managing the A.T. corridor lands outside established parks and forests to the Appalachian Trail Conference. The Conference and its clubs retain primary responsibility for maintaining the footpath, too. A new, more comprehensive 10-year agreement was signed in 1994.

Trail geology

Lynn S. Fichter, Professor, Department of Geology and Environmental Science, James Madison University

Why aren't the Appalachians as high as other American mountain systems?

In a word: erosion. The modern Appalachians are not even true "mountains" in the geologic sense, but the incompletely eroded remnants of an ancient, 30,000-foot-high mountain range, the Alleghanian, that formed about 300 million years ago. In contrast, the modern Appalachians are from 3,000 to 6,000 feet high. During the continental collision that formed the Alleghanian mountains, the ancient rocks we know as today's Appalachians were folded and faulted while deep underground.

So, what are we seeing when we look at today's Appalachians?

We see five geologic divisions (called *provinces*) that run roughly parallel to the Atlantic coast. Each province contains rocks that formed at different times in geologic history. They are, from east to west, the coastal plain, Piedmont, Blue Ridge, Ridge and Valley Province, and Allegheny Plateau.

What caused them to form?

The Appalachian rocks you see on and from the Trail are the result of the opening and closing of ocean basins. In the opening phase, a huge land mass called a supercontinent rifts into continent-sized fragments. As the continents spread apart, an ocean basin opens. The land and undersea areas along the edges of the new continent are called *divergent continental margins* (DCMs). Today's Atlantic seaboard is just such a margin, while the great valleys west of the Trail contain the remnants of an ancient DCM that formed about 500 million years ago.

What happens when an ocean basin starts to close?

When an ocean basin begins to close, and continents converge together, *subduction zones* form in the basin, where one part of the ocean floor is forced under another part, or under a continental plate, forming mountains. Such a zone under the edge of a continent builds mountains like today's Andes, at the ocean's edge. Such a zone in midocean forms a *volcanic arc* of islands, like those of modern-day Japan. As the ocean basin continues to close, eventually the volcanic arc collides with a continent, building more mountains. Finally, mountains build when the ocean basin closes completely and two continental plates collide, creating the next supercontinent.

What are the geologic events recorded in the Appalachians?

The Appalachian mountains give us a geological record stretching back 1.8 billion years and containing the closing half of one cycle, which built an ancient supercontinent (called "Rodinia"), then a full cycle that built a more recent supercontinent ("Pangaea"), and finally the opening half of a third cycle that has produced the modern-day Atlantic seaboard.

What was the first Appalachian mountain-building event?

The *Grenville orogeny*, one billion years ago, is the oldest of which we have a geologic record. The ocean floor was pushed under the North American continent, building Andean-sized mountains, followed by the continent-to-continent collision that created the Rodinia supercontinent. On the Trail, you spend much of your time crossing rocks formed during the Grenville orogeny (mountain-building event).

What were the other mountain-buiding events?

For half a billion years, eastern North America lay in the center of a supercontinent. But, about 600 million years ago, that continent rifted apart to form what geologists call the "proto-Atlantic" (or Iapitus) ocean and a divergent continental margin. The rocks left over from that are preserved today in the great valleys west of the Trail. During the closing phase of the cycle, there were three more orogenies: the *Taconic* (a volcanic arc collision), the *Acadian* (a volcanic arc/microcontinent collision), and the *Alleghanian* (when what is now Africa collided with eastern North America, closed the proto-Atlantic, and formed Pangaea). The modern Atlantic Ocean and its present-day divergent continental margin began forming 200 million years ago.

How high were the ancient mountains?

During the Grenville and Alleghanian orogenies, Andean- and Himalayan-sized mountains formed. During the smaller Taconic and Acadian orogenies, mountains formed that were the size of today's Alps or Rockies—14,000 to 15,000 feet high.

How are each the five Appalachian provinces different?

- The *coastal plain* is the newest and youngest. There are no mountain-built structures or rocks here, just sediment brought down to the coast from inland. The A.T. never descends to the coastal plain.

■ The *Piedmont* is mostly "exotic," meaning that it contains volcanic arcs and fragments of ocean floor brought to North America from other places in the world. They are severely deformed, metamorphosed, and eroded down to their deep roots. The Trail in New Hampshire and Maine is actually part of this region, although it crosses some of the Trail's highest mountains that might not appear at first to fit the definition of "piedmont" (foothills).

■ The *Blue Ridge* contains the eroded roots of the Grenville mountains, which once covered the eastern part of the continent from Texas to Quebec. Long sections of the Trail follow the Blue Ridge.

■ The *Ridge and Valley Province* is made of folded and faulted sedimentary rocks and contains rocks from the proto-Atlantic, as well as sediments eroded from the Taconic and Acadian mountains. The Trail in the mid-Atlantic enters this province.

■ Finally, farthest west, the *Allegheny Plateau* is made of sedimentary rocks and contains virtually a complete sedimentary record of everything since the proto-Atlantic began forming.

Why does so much of the Trail follow the Blue Ridge?

The Blue Ridge acts like a backbone for the Appalachian region and thus for the Trail. Not only is it the central province, its rocks are the oldest and stand the highest, primarily because they are still gently rising. Looking east into the Piedmont, we see the eroded remains of the Taconic and Acadian mountains. Looking west into the Ridge and Valley Province, we see the sediments eroded from those mountains that were deposited in deep basins existing there at the time. All this must be in the geological imagination, of course; none of what we see today resembles the ancient landscapes in topography, vegetation, or climate.

Why are there so many long, folded ridges today?

The modern landscape is largely the result of the Alleghenian orogeny, which folded and faulted all the previous rocks and shuffled them like a deck of cards. Virtually no rocks exposed today are where they originally formed, except for the Allegheny Plateau, west of the A.T. During the Alleghanian orogeny, Africa rode up over the edge of North America, peeled the rocks off in layers thousands of feet thick and shoved them dozens of miles inland from their original locations. The faults and folds all run parallel to each other, and, where they bring soft rocks to the surface, erosion is easy and valleys form. The ridges are made of more erosion-resistant rocks.

What rocks are those divisions made of?

The core rocks in the Blue Ridge are *batholiths,* coarse-grained, mostly light-colored rocks formed from molten materials deep in the roots of the Grenville mountains. In places in Virginia, they are overlain by 600-million-year-old basalt lava flows (dark green) ejected over the eroded batholiths when the proto-Atlantic ocean opened. In the Smokies, many of the rocks began as sedimentary rocks of about the same age as the lava flows, moved westward from the Piedmont regions during the Alleghanian orogeny, and metamorphosed by heat and pressure. East of the Blue Ridge, and in northern New England, the rocks are all igneous and metamorphic. They include igneous batholiths (such as granite) and lava flows associated with several ancient volcanic arcs, or rocks deposited on the sides of the volcanic arcs. Looking west from the Blue Ridge, the rocks are all sedimentary. The Roanoke Valley, Shenandoah/Page valleys, and Great Valley of Maryland and Pennsylvania, for example, are underlain largely by limestones of the proto-Atlantic continental margin. The far mountain ridges west of the Shenandoah and Great Valley are mostly sandstones and shales from the Taconic and Acadian orogenies. All of those rocks are *thrust faulted;* that is, they consist of a series of "sheets"—a mile or more thick—that have been shoved over each other and stacked.

Were the Appalachians affected by the Ice Age?

Repeatedly. The Trail's lowest point is where it crosses the Hudson River, a scant 124 feet above sea level. Ice Age glaciers carved the Hudson River Valley, the only fjord on the Trail. From the Delaware Water Gap north, you enter glacial country from the Ice Age that ended about 20,000 years ago, and, the farther north you go, the more glacial evidence you can see. New England mountains are typically scraped nearly bare on top, with swampy, fertile valleys where soil was deposited when the ice melted. Large *erratics*, boulders that the glaciers carried miles from the rock formations they were broken away from, appear regularly in this region. *Cirques,* carved by growing glaciers, rubble hills (*terminal moraines*) formed where glaciers stopped advancing, and long gravely mounds (*eskers*) formed by deposits from melting ice are other features. The Trail runs along some rocky ridges where the scratches and scrapes of moving ice are still visible.

Wildlife along the A.T.

How "wild" is the A.T.?

The well-known plaque at Springer Mountain in Georgia describes the A.T. as "a footpath for those who seek fellowship with the wilderness." What does that mean? The Trail will indeed take you deep into some of the wildest and most remote woodlands of the eastern United States. But true "wilderness," in the sense of untouched wild country, is rare, even on the A.T. Much of the land that the Trail follows was once farmland—even the steep, stony, remote slopes—and nearly all of it has been logged at some time during the last four centuries. Except for bears, bobcats, and coyotes, most large natural predators have been exterminated.

In the twentieth century, though, much of the formerly settled land was incorporated into state and national parks and forests. On that land, forests and wildlife have returned. As you walk through what seems like primeval wilderness, you're likely to run across old stone walls or abandoned logging roads or the foundations of nineteenth-century homesteads. The federal government has designated some of those areas as protected wilderness areas, which strictly limits the ways in which they can be used. Today, the mountains teem with creatures of all sorts, from microbes to moose. To the casual hiker who knows only the woods of a suburban park, it can seem very wild indeed.

One good way to look at the "wilderness" of the A.T. is as a series of long, skinny islands of wildness, surrounded by a sea of populated valleys inhabited by working farms and suburban communities. In the vast national forests of the South and the spreading timberlands of northern New England, those "islands" are somewhat broader. But, even in its wildest places, the A.T. hiker is rarely more than a strenuous day's walk from the nearest highway or community.

What large animals might I see?

Moose, the largest animal that hikers encounter along the Trail (often weighing in at more than 1,000 pounds), inhabit deep woodlands and wetlands from Massachusetts north, especially in New Hampshire and Maine. White-tailed deer can be found along the entire length of the Trail. Elk have been reintroduced to Pennsylvania, North Carolina, and Tennessee. Black bears have been spotted in all Trail states and are especially common in Georgia, North Carolina, Tennessee, Virginia, Pennsylvania, and New Jersey. Wild boars live in the Great Smoky Mountains National Park. Bobcats and coyotes are stealthy residents along most of the route of the Trail, though they're rarely seen. Fishers, otters, and beavers are occasionally reported by hikers.

What small animals might I see?

By far the most familiar will be mice, chipmunks, rabbits, and squirrels, but foxes, raccoons, opossums, skunks, groundhogs, porcupines, bats, weasels, shrews, minks, and muskrats are also common. Tree frogs and bullfrogs inhabit wet areas in warm weather, lizards scurry along rocks and fallen logs, snakes (both poisonous and nonpoisonous) are common south of New England, and streams and ponds are home to salamanders, bass, trout, bream, sunfish, catfish, and crayfish.

Which animals are dangerous?

Few A.T. hikers encounter aggressive animals, but any wild animal will fight if cornered or handled roughly—even timid animals such as deer can be quite dangerous in those circumstances. The large wild animals most likely to be aggressive include moose (during rutting season) and black bears (especially mother bears with cubs). Mountain lions, which have stalked people in western states, have long been rumored to have returned to the Appalachians, but so far scientists have not been able to confirm any sightings in mountains that the A.T. traverses.

When disturbed or stepped on, many other creatures will strike back aggressively, inflicting painful wounds or poisonous stings. These include timber rattlesnakes and copperheads, water moccasins, hornets, wasps, yellow jackets, Africanized bees, and black widow and brown recluse spiders. Foxes, bats, raccoons, and other small animals susceptible to rabies may bite when suffering from infection. Mice, though not aggressive, may transmit diseases, and biting insects such as mosquitoes and ticks can infect hikers with bacteria. Hikers in more populated sections of the Trail may also encounter aggressive dogs.

What rare or endangered animal species might I see?

Birders might spot rare species such as the Bicknell's thrush, hermit thrush, gray-cheeked thrush, northern raven, olive-sided flycatcher, black-billed cuckoo, spruce grouse, bay-breasted warbler, cerulean warbler, blackburnian warbler, magnolia warbler, blackpoll warbler, alder flycatcher, rusty blackbird, Swainson's warbler, yellow-bellied sapsucker, winter wren, redbreasted nuthatch, sharp-shinned hawk, northern saw-whet owl, golden eagle, peregrine falcon, merlin, bald eagle, and Cooper's hawk.

Harder to find, but also present, are the Carolina northern flying squirrel, Virginia northern flying squirrel, rock vole, Allegheny wood rat, eastern wood rat, water shrew, and fence lizard. The black bear and eastern timber rattlesnake, though not uncommon along the Trail, are on the rare species list. You may also find a number of rare crustaceans, reptiles, and amphibians, including the zig-zag salamander, northern cricket frog, triangle floater mussel, Jefferson salamander, Appalachian brook crayfish, wood turtle, broadhead skink, pigmy salamander, shovelnose salamander, Shenandoah salamander, Weller's salmander, and squawfoot mussel.

What birds will I see in the Appalachians that I might not see at my backyard feeder?

Birds whose summer range is normally far to the north of where most A.T. hikers live are often found in the mountains, where the altitude makes the climate resemble that of Canada. Insect-eating birds such as whippoorwills, flycatchers, and swallows rarely show up in back yards but are common along the Trail. The songs of deep-woods birds such as the ovenbird, kinglet, veery, pewee, and red-eyed-vireo will provide an ongoing chorus for summer hikers. Pileated woodpeckers hammer deliberately on dead trees. Large game birds, such as wild turkey, ruffed grouse, and spruce grouse, forage on the forest floor and surprise hikers as they burst into flight. Many hikers linger to admire the soaring acrobatics of ravens, vultures, hawks, eagles, and falcons on the thermals and updrafts along the rocky crests of the mountains.

Trees and wild plants along the A.T.

How old are the Appalachian forests?

The forests of the Appalachians have been logged heavily for three centuries. Photos from the late nineteenth and early twentieth centuries show many areas almost completely stripped of trees. Many Trail areas were open farmland or pastureland in the 1700s and early 1800s. Lumber is still harvested in national forests and privately owned timberlands along the Trail. Although today's mountains are heavily forested again, it is mostly "second-growth" timber, except in a few isolated coves of "old-growth" forest that date back to pre-Colonial times.

Forest that has grown back from burning or clearing through successive stages to the point at which it reaches a fairly steady state, with dominant full-grown trees, is known as a "climax forest." Several different climax forests appear along the A.T., and they are not mutually exclusive—different types can be found on the same mountain. The kind you encounter will depend on where you are, on what type of soil is underfoot, and the climate. The climate often depends on how high the mountains are—the taller they are, the more "northern" (or *boreal*) the climate.

What kinds of forests will I encounter along the Trail?

- The *mixed deciduous forest* (also called the *Southern hardwood forest*) dominates Trail lands south of New England and the foothills of the southern mountains. Various kinds of broad-leafed trees are dominant, and the understory of small trees and shrubs is profuse. Oaks and hickories are the most common large trees, with maples and beeches evident in more northerly sections; some sproutings of chestnuts (a species that predominated until a blight devastated it early in the twentieth century) can be found as well. Understory trees such as redbuds, dogwoods, striped maples, and American hollies are common, as are shrubs such as witch hazel, pawpaws, and mountain pepperbushes.

- The *southern Appalachian forest,* found above the foothills from Georgia to central Virginia, contains more tree species than any other forest in North America and actually takes in a range of different forest types that can vary dramatically according to elevation. Climax hardwood forests of basswood, birch, maple, beech, tuliptree, ash, and magnolia can be found in some coves, while above about 4,000 feet the climax forests are typically spruce, fir, and hemlock, particularly on the wetter western slopes. Old-growth forest can be found in isolated parts of the Great Smoky Mountains National Park. Oak forests often predominate on the eastern faces of the mountains, which do not typically receive as much moisture. Pines and oaks may mix on some slopes. At higher elevations, the understory is less varied: Shrubs of mountain laurel and rhododendron form nearly impenetrable thickets that are densest where conditions are wettest.

■ The *transition forest* tends to be wetter and more northerly than the mixed deciduous forest. Hikers marveling at the colors of a New England fall are admiring the transition forest. It extends across the hillsides and lowlands of the north and reaches down into the high country of the southern Appalachians. It appears as a mosaic of spruce, fir, hemlock, pine, birch, maple, basswood, and beech forests. The substory of transition forest tends to be more open, with ferns, shrubs of elderberry, hazel, and bush honeysuckle, and often a thick carpet of evergreen needles covers the ground under the trees. Conifers tend to predominate at the higher elevations.

■ The northern, or *boreal forest,* is the largest North American forest. Most of it is in Canada and Alaska, but A.T. hikers encounter it while traversing the highest ridges of the southern Appalachians and the coniferous uplands of northern New England. Pines and hemlocks characterize its southern reaches, while dwarfed spruces and firs (known as *krummholz* or *taiga*) grow at treeline in New Hampshire and Maine, just as they grow at the borders of the arctic lands farther north. In between is a spruce-fir climax forest. Evergreens such as white pine, red pine, white spruce, balsam fir, black spruce, and jack pine predominate, but hardwoods such as aspen and birch are mixed in as well. The ground of the boreal forest is typically thin and muddy, with little in the way of an understory and sphagnum bogs surrounded by a wide variety of aquatic plants, ferns, subalpine plants, blueberry bushes, and mountain maple and ash shrubs.

What wildflowers can I look for, and when will I see them?

Among the small joys of hiking the Trail are the wildflowers that grow along the way. Some poke their heads out of the forest duff in late winter and are gone by the time the spreading canopy of late spring trees blocks out the sun. Some cluster near the edges of clearings in midsummer, while others hide in the deep shade. And, still others blossom amid the falling leaves and early snows of the Appalachian fall.

Winter/early spring—First to bloom in swampy areas most years is the maroon-colored cowl that shelters the tiny, foul-smelling flowers of *skunk cabbage*, which may appear while snow is still on the ground. In March and April, along the high, dry ridges, the delicate starbursts of *bloodroot* appear, along with the corncob-like clusters of *squaw root* on fallen oak trees, the graceful lily-like *dogtooth violet,* the white bunches of *early saxifrage*, fanlike purple clusters of *dwarf iris* in southern sections, the pink-purple flowers and liver-shaped leaves of *hepatica*, the delicate white *rue anemone*, the bee-buzzing carpets of *fringed phacelia* in the south, and the waxy pink *trailing arbutus* farther north.

Spring/early summer—During May and June, as the tree canopy shades the forest floor, the variety of wildflowers blooming along the A.T. becomes too extensive to keep track of. The bubblegum scent and orange blooms of *flame azalea* shrubs burst out in the southern Appalachians, along with the white and pink blossoms of its close relatives, *mountain laurel* and *rhododendron*. The garlicky *wild leek*, or *ramp*, flowers in early summer. Hikers may spot the green tubes of *jack-in-the-pulpit*, dove-like red clusters of *wild columbine*, vessel-like orchid blossom of *pink lady's-slipper*, spade-leaved *trillium*, bright blue of *viper's bugloss*, the blue-violet of *spiderwort* in sunny clearings, *black cohosh*'s delicate cone of tiny blooms, and, in the cold bogs of the northern states, the white blossoms of *labrador tea* and the pink pentagons of *bog laurel*.

Late summer—The heat of July and August in the Appalachians coaxes blossoms from a number of mountain shrubs, shade plants, and meadow plants. The *wintergreen* shrub blooms white in oak forests, the white starbursts of *tall meadow rue* appear near open fields, the white petals of the bug-trapping *sundew* appear in wet areas, *mountain cranberry*'s small bell-like pink blossoms appear in New England, the white-and-yellow sunbursts of *oxeye daisy* grow along hedgerows, and the greenish-white clusters of *wild sarsaparilla* appear in the dry, open woods. In the mid-Atlantic states, the understory becomes a waist-deep sea of *wood nettle*, the delicate white flowers of which belie unpleasant stinging hairs that bristle from the stems and leaves; the succulent stalks of *jewel-weed*, which has a pale yellow flower, often sprout nearby, and their juice can help ease the sting and itch of the nettles.

Fall and early winter—Certain wildflowers continue blooming late into the fall along the A.T., disappearing from the woods about the same time hikers do. *Goldenrod* spreads across open fields in September, about the time the leaves start changing color. The intricate white discs of *Queen Anne's lace* adorn ditches and roadsides until late in the year. Other common fall wildflowers include *aster, wood sorrel, monkshood,* and *butter-and-eggs.*

Can I eat wild plants I find?
You could eat certain plants, but, in keeping with the principles of Leave No Trace, you probably shouldn't. Leave the wild blueberries and rasp-berries and blackberries of summer for the birds and bears. Resist the temptation to spice up your noodles with ramps in the spring. "Chicken of the woods" mushrooms should stay in the woods. Wild watercress belongs in a stream, not a salad. Rather than brewing your own ginseng or sassafras tea from wild roots, visit the supermarket in town. Many ed-ible plants along the A.T. are rare and endangered, and harvesting them is illegal. Even when the flora are plentiful, remember that the fauna of the Appalachians have no option other than to forage for it; you do.

What rare or endangered plant species might I see?
Most of the federally listed plant species (threatened or endangered) along the Appalachian Trail are found in the high country of the southern Ap-palachians or the alpine environments of northern New England. There are too many to list here, but typical of those in the southern Appalachians is the *spreading avens,* a plant with fan-shaped leaves and small, yellow flowers that grows in rock crevices. Although *bluets* are common along the A.T., a subspecies called *Roan Mountain bluet* is found in only nine

sites there—the only known sites in the world. *Gray's lily* is found only on the high balds near Roan Mountain. Although *goldenrod* is plentiful along the Trail and sometimes considered something of a pest, one rare subspecies, the *Blue Ridge goldenrod,* is known to exist only on one cliff in North Carolina. Similarly, many of the plants at and above treeline in New England, such as *Robbins cinquefoil,* are extremely vulnerable to damage from hikers wandering off the A.T. Below treeline, plants such as the *small whorled pogonia,* an orchid, are threatened by development.

The how and why of Trail construction

Who decides which route the Trail takes?

A local Trail-maintaining club, in consultation with the Appalachian Trail Conference and the government agency responsible for managing the land in question, determines the route that the footpath follows over a section. According to the National Scenic Trails Act that authorized the A.T., the goal is to expose the walker to "the maximum outdoor recreation potential and for the conservation and enjoyment of the nationally significant scenic, historic, natural or cultural qualities of the area." In plain language, that means routing the Trail in such a way that walkers have the chance to encounter and appreciate the wildlife, geography, and geology, as well as the historical and natural context of the Appalachians, while merging with, exploring, and harmonizing with the mountain environment.

How is today's A.T. different from the original Trail?

When the A.T. was first built, the main goal was a continuous, marked route, which often meant connecting existing footpaths and woods roads. Long sections of "roadwalks" linked the footpaths. Where no existing routes were available, Trail builders marked out new ones, cleared brush, and painted blazes. But, that was about it, and, for many years, when few people knew about or hiked the Trail, it was enough. Beginning in the 1960s, though, two things happened: The A.T. became a part of the national park system, and the numbers of people using it began skyrocketing. With increased use, mud and erosion became problems. As the Trail was moved away from existing footpaths and roads and onto new paths planned and built especially for the A.T. on federal land,

Trail builders began "hardening" the path and designing it to stand up to heavier use.

What causes the Trail to deteriorate?

Erosion can damage the footpath quickly. The mineral soil of the footpath is made of very fine particles bound together by clay that, once broken from the ground by boots and hiking poles, is easily washed away by fast-flowing water. (Water moving at two miles per hour has sixty-four times more ability to carry soil particles than water moving at one mile per hour.) Trail builders work to separate water from the treadway. Where that is not possible, they try to slow it down. Since water in rivulets or ruts flows faster than water flowing across the Trail in sheets, trail builders try to channel water off the part that hikers walk on. Where they can't, they slant the path outward so that water will stay "thin" and flow slowly off the sides in a sheet, rather than becoming "thick" and channeling down the middle of the Trail.

Why are parts of the Trail routed over narrow log walkways?

Believe it or not, it's not to keep your feet dry. The goal is to protect the land, not your nice, new boots. Bog bridges, also called "puncheon," allow the Trail to take hikers into an important part of the mountain environment without turning such ecologically sensitive swamp areas into hopeless quagmires, disrupting plant and animal life there. The Trail is supposed to "wear lightly on the land," and this is one way to do so. Walkways may be built on piles driven into the ground, or they may "float" on boggy ground; in both cases, the wetlands are disturbed much less than they would be by mud holes that widen every time a hiker tries to skirt the edges.

Why does the Trail zigzag up steep mountains?

When it was first marked, the Trail often climbed steep slopes by the most direct route, and older parts of today's Trail still tend to have the steepest sections. But, water runs faster down a steeper trail and erodes it more quickly. In recent years, many sections have been rerouted so that the Trail ascends by way of "sidehill" that slants up a mountainside and "switchbacks" that zigzag across its steepest faces. Again, it isn't done to make the Trail easier for hikers, although that's sometimes the effect, but rather to make the footpath itself more durable and less subject to erosion.

How does the Trail cross creeks and rivers?

Bridges take the Trail across all its major river crossings, except for the Kennebec River in Maine (where hikers ferry across in canoes). Most, such as the Bear Mountain Bridge across the Hudson in New York, are highway bridges; a few others, such as the James River Foot Bridge in Virginia, are built especially for foot travelers. A few large creeks require fording, but most are crossed by footbridges or stepping stones. Small streams may require fording when spring floods submerge the rocks and stepping stones that lead across them.

Why are there so many logs and rock barriers in the path?

Unless the logs result from a "blowdown" (a fallen tree) or the rocks from a rockslide, they're probably water-diversion devices, such as waterbars or check dams that have been added to older, eroding sections of the Trail. Avoid stepping on them, if possible: Not only can they be slippery (particularly the logs), but they will last longer if you step over them.

Why is the Trail so rocky?

As you may have read in the section of this guide devoted to geology, the Appalachians are the product of erosion, which tends to strip away soil and leave rocks on the surface. Since rocky sections offer a durable surface and often provide spectacular views for hikers, Trail designers don't hesitate to route the footpath along them. This is particularly true from central Virginia through Connecticut and eastern New Hampshire through Maine; many older sections of the Trail are routed along ridgelines. Typically, the A.T. will climb a ridge on smoother "sidehill" Trail and then follow a rocky ridgeline for some distance, before descending again.

Summary of Distances

North–South
CUMULATIVE
MILES

South–North
CUMULATIVE
MILES

Connecticut Section Five (New York Section One)

0.0	0.0	Conn. 341	11.5	11.5
0.3	0.3	Mt. Algo Lean-to	11.2	11.2
3.2	3.2	Schaghticoke Mountain Campsite	8.3	8.3
3.8	3.8	Indian Rocks	7.7	7.7
7.1	7.1	Schaghticoke Road	4.4	4.4
8.5	8.5	Ten Mile River Campsite	3.0	3.0
8.7	8.7	Ten Mile River Lean-to	2.8	2.8
10.8	10.8	Conn. 55	0.7	0.7
11.5	11.5	Hoyt Road, N.Y./Conn. State Line	0.0	0.0

New York Section Two

0.0	0.0	Hoyt Road, N.Y./Conn. State Line	160.9	7.1
1.0	1.0	Duell Hollow Road	159.9	6.1
1.2	1.2	Wiley Shelter	159.7	5.9
1.6	1.6	Leather Hill Road	159.3	5.5
6.9	6.9	Hurds Corners Road	154.0	0.2
7.1	7.1	N.Y. 22	153.8	0.0

New York Section Three

0.0	7.1	N.Y. 22	153.8	7.4
2.4	9.5	County 20 (West Dover Road)	151.4	5.0
3.1	10.2	Telephone Pioneers Shelter	150.7	4.3
3.4	10.5	West Mountain Summit	150.4	4.0
3.9	11.0	Penny Road	149.9	3.5
7.4	14.5	N.Y. 55	146.4	0.0

New York Section Four

0.0	14.5	N.Y. 55	146.4	7.2
0.3	14.8	Old N.Y. 55	146.1	6.9
2.2	16.7	Depot Hill Road	144.2	5.0
3.3	17.8	Morgan Stewart Memorial Shelter	143.1	3.9
3.4	17.9	Mt. Egbert Summit	143.0	3.8
5.8	20.3	I-84 Overpass, Mountain Top Road	140.6	1.4
7.2	21.7	N.Y. 52	139.2	0.0

New York Section Five

0.0	21.7	N.Y. 52	139.2	4.8
1.6	23.3	Hosner Mountain Road	137.6	3.2
4.8	26.5	Taconic State Parkway	134.4	0.0

New York Section Six

0.0	26.5	Taconic State Parkway	134.4	7.3
0.3	26.8	Hortontown Road, RPH Shelter	134.1	7.0
1.6	28.1	Shenandoah Tenting Area	132.8	5.7
2.7	29.2	Long Hill Road	131.7	4.6
3.1	29.6	Shenandoah Mountain Summit	131.3	4.2
7.3	33.8	N.Y. 301, Canopus Lake	127.1	0.0

New York Section Seven

0.0	33.8	N.Y. 301, Canopus Lake	127.1	7.4
2.1	35.9	Sunk Mine Road	125.0	5.3
3.7	37.5	Dennytown Road Campsites	123.4	3.7
7.4	41.2	Canopus Hill Road	119.7	0.0

North–South   **South–North**

New York Section Eight

0.0	41.2	Canopus Hill Road	119.7	5.0
0.7	41.9	Canopus Hill Summit	119.0	4.3
1.7	42.9	Chapman Road, Old Albany Post Road	118.0	3.3
2.5	43.7	Denning Hill Summit	117.2	2.5
4.4	45.6	Old West Point Road	115.3	0.6
5.0	46.2	U.S. 9, N.Y. 403	114.7	0.0

New York Section Nine

0.0	46.2	U.S. 9, N.Y. 403	114.7	5.8
3.4	49.6	South Mountain Pass Road	111.3	2.4
3.6	49.8	Hemlock Springs Campsite	111.1	2.2
5.1	51.3	N.Y. 9D, Westchester–Putnam County Line	109.6	0.7
5.8	52.0	Bear Mountain Bridge (west end)	108.9	0.0

New York Section Ten

0.0	52.0	Bear Mountain Bridge (west end)	108.9	13.1
0.8	52.8	Bear Mountain Inn	108.1	12.3
2.6	54.6	Bear Mountain Summit	106.3	10.5
4.2	56.2	Seven Lakes Drive	104.7	8.9
5.8	57.8	West Mountain Shelter	103.1	7.3
6.8	58.8	Palisades Interstate Parkway	102.1	6.3
7.5	59.5	Black Mountain	101.4	5.6
8.9	60.9	William Brien Memorial Shelter	100.0	4.2
10.9	62.9	Seven Lakes Drive	98.0	2.2
13.1	65.1	Arden Valley Road	95.8	0.0

North–South			**South–North**	

New York Section Eleven

0.0	65.1	Arden Valley Road	95.8	5.5
1.1	66.2	Fingerboard Shelter	94.7	4.4
3.2	68.3	Lemon Squeezer	92.6	2.3
5.5	70.6	N.Y. 17	90.3	0.0

New York Section Twelve

0.0	70.6	N.Y. 17	90.3	12.0
1.1	71.7	Arden Mountain Summit	89.2	10.9
1.8	72.4	Orange Turnpike	88.5	10.2
3.2	73.8	East Mombasha Road	87.1	8.8
4.9	75.5	West Mombasha Road	85.4	7.1
6.1	76.7	Mombasha High Point	84.2	5.9
8.1	78.7	Fitzgerald Falls	82.2	3.9
8.4	79.0	Lakes Road	81.9	3.6
9.9	80.5	Wildcat Shelter	80.4	2.1
10.2	80.8	Cat Rocks	80.1	1.8
10.7	81.3	Eastern Pinnacles	79.6	1.3
12.0	82.6	N.Y. 17A	78.3	0.0

New York Section Thirteen

0.0	82.6	N.Y. 17A	78.3	5.9
5.5	88.1	Prospect Rock	72.8	0.4
5.9	88.5	State Line Trail	72.4	0.0

North–South				South–North	

New Jersey Section One

0.0	88.5	State Line Trail	72.4	9.3
1.1	89.6	Long House Creek	71.3	8.2
2.2	90.7	Long House Road	70.2	7.1
3.6	92.1	Warwick Turnpike	68.8	5.7
4.0	92.5	Wawayanda Shelter	68.4	5.3
5.1	93.6	Double Kill Bridge	67.3	4.2
6.2	94.7	Barrett Road	66.2	3.1
7.9	96.4	Wawayanda Mountain	64.5	1.4
9.3	97.8	N.J. 94	63.1	0.0

New Jersey Section Two

0.0	97.8	N.J. 94	63.1	10.8
2.3	100.1	County 517	60.8	8.5
3.8	101.6	County 565	59.3	7.0
5.0	102.8	Pochuck Mountain Summit	58.1	5.8
6.5	104.3	Pochuck Mountain Shelter	56.6	4.3
7.0	104.8	Lake Wallkill Road	56.1	3.8
9.3	107.1	Wallkill River Bridge	53.8	1.5
10.8	108.6	N.J. 284	52.3	0.0

New Jersey Section Three

0.0	108.6	N.J. 284	52.3	9.8
1.0	109.6	Lott Road (Jersey Avenue)	51.3	8.8
1.9	110.5	Unionville Road (County 651)	50.4	7.9
3.2	111.8	Goodrich Road	49.1	6.6
4.2	112.8	Gemmer Road	48.1	5.6
6.0	114.6	Courtwright Road	46.3	3.8
6.8	115.4	County 519	45.5	3.0
8.1	116.7	High Point Shelter	44.2	1.7
9.8	118.4	N.J. 23	42.5	0.0

North–South   **South–North**

New Jersey Section Four

0.0	118.4	N.J. 23	42.5	14.3
2.6	121.0	Rutherford Shelter	39.9	11.7
5.3	123.7	Deckertown Turnpike	37.2	9.0
5.5	123.9	Mashipacong Shelter	37.0	8.8
8.1	126.5	Crigger Road	34.4	6.2
8.9	127.3	Sunrise Mountain Summit	33.6	5.4
11.3	129.7	Gren Anderson Shelter	31.2	3.0
12.4	130.8	Culver Fire Tower	30.1	1.9
14.3	132.7	U.S. 206	28.2	0.0

New Jersey Section Five

0.0	132.7	U.S. 206	28.2	14.5
3.6	136.3	Brink Road Shelter	24.6	10.9
5.8	138.5	Rattlesnake Mountain Summit	22.4	8.7
7.7	140.4	Buttermilk Falls Trail	20.5	6.8
10.6	143.3	Blue Mountain Lakes Road	17.6	3.9
14.5	147.2	Millbrook-Blairstown Road	13.7	0.0

New Jersey Section Six

0.0	147.2	Millbrook-Blairstown Road	13.7	13.7
1.0	148.2	Catfish Fire Tower	12.7	12.7
3.4	150.6	Camp Road	10.3	10.3
7.8	155.0	Sunfish Pond	5.9	5.9
9.1	156.3	Backpacker Site (no water)	4.6	4.6
12.2	159.4	Dunnfield Creek Parking Area	1.5	1.5
13.7	160.9	Delaware Water Gap, Pa.	0.0	0.0

Index

Picture credits

Photographs on the following pages are courtesy of:

i G.W. Szelc; ii–iii Frank Howd; 4 and 6–7 Appalachian Trail Conference; 25 Mike Warren; 27 Appalachian Trail Conference; 30–31 and 35 Mike Warren; 39 Constance Durnan; 47 Andrew Fay; 53 Appalachian Trail Conference; 61 Daniel Chazin; 71 and 77 Mike Warren; 89 Francy Ogan; 95 Joe Haitmann; 105 Mike Warren; 109 Cole Thompson; 113 and 125 G.W. Szelc; 129 Appalachian Trail Conference; 131 Richard Frear; 134 and 141 Mike Warren; 144–145 Chris Myers; 149 Mike Warren; 152 Appalachian Trail Conference; 161 Mike Warren; 174 Appalachian Trail Conference; 176 Kathleen Mallow-Sager; 181 Michael Bruce; 185 Appalachian Trail Conference; 189 Joan Myer; 197 and 200 Appalachian Trail Conference; 209 Lou Le Blanc; 213 Wayne Gross; and 219 Mike Warren.

The Appalachian Trail Conference

ATC's administrative headquarters is located in Harpers Ferry, West Virginia. Membership services, publications and merchandise sales, and requests for information about the Trail are all handled there. The public Information Center is also located there. Regular business hours are 9 a.m.–5 p.m. EST, Monday–Friday.

P. O. Box 807
799 Washington Street
Harpers Ferry, WV 25425-0807
Phone: (304) 535-6331
Fax: (304) 535-2667

The Ultimate Appalachian Trail Store
For customer service, call toll-free to (888) AT-STORE during weekday business hours (9 a.m.–5 p.m. EST).
<www.atctrailstore.org>

Frequently Requested E-mail Addresses
Trail & hiking questions: <info@appalachiantrail.org>
ATC membership: <membership@appalachiantrail.org>
The Ultimate A.T. Store: <sales@appalachiantrail.org>
Editor, ATC publications: <editor@appalachiantrail.org>
Volunteer Trail crew program: <crews@appalachiantrail.org>
Ridgerunner program: <ridgerunner@appalachiantrail.org>
Reporting an incident: <incident@appalachiantrail.org>

The New York–New Jersey Trail Conference

156 Ramapo Valley Road (U.S. 202)
Mahwah, NJ 07430
Office hours: Monday–Friday, 11:00 am–5:30 pm
Phone: (201) 512-9348, or leave a message any time.
Fax: (201) 512-9012
Orders of maps and books: (201) 512-9348
E-mail: <info@nynjtc.org>
Office: <office@nynjtc.org>
Hikers' Market Place: <www.nynjtc.org>